Sex during pregnancy
and after
childbirth

by

Sylvia Close
SANC Med. and Surg. (Hons)
SANC Midwifery (Hons)
Athlone Mothercraft Certificate in Infant Dietetics

THORSONS PUBLISHERS LIMITED
Wellingborough, Northamptonshire

First published 1984

© SYLVIA CLOSE 1984

British Library Cataloguing in Publication Data

Close, Sylvia
   Sex during pregnancy and after childbirth.
   1. Pregnancy   2. Sex
   I. Title
   612'6   RG525

   ISBN 0-7225-0929-4

Printed and bound in Great Britain by
Whitstable Litho Ltd., Whitstable, Kent

Contents

Foreword

Some years ago a best-selling book appeared on the market with a lot of publicity. Its title was *Everything You Always Wanted to Know About Sex but Were Afraid to Ask*. If the word 'ashamed' is substituted for 'afraid' you have a situation that confronts very many women in antenatal clinics. Women are just ashamed to ask questions about sex during pregnancy. They feel that the doctors or nurses in the clinics will think that there is something indecent about the question, or they will think that the doctors and midwives are far too busy dealing with things that have gone wrong to spend time on semi-frivolous questions.

The question of sex in pregnancy and after the baby is born is not frivolous at all. Sex is an extremely important component of partners' lives and many couples argue about sex during pregnancy. Many men are frightened of hurting the baby. Many women feel that sex is an intrusion on something between the baby and themselves. On the other hand very many women want to be loved more during pregnancy than at any other time in order to overcome what they think is a state of ugliness. Some men, it is true, do find later pregnancy in their wives off-putting. Others want to be more protective and want sex but are themselves afraid of what it may do.

Sylvia Close has a great gift for writing. She has a wonderful sense of being able to find out what men and women want; and I purposely put men before women for this book because, although I dare say more women than men will buy it, I am equally sure as many men as women will want to read it.

The book contains much more than simple answers to the simple question of 'Can we do it?'. It contains an account of some of the things that may not be quite right during the pregnancy, such as vaginal infections. It explains how intercourse may matter in the case of women with infections or how these infections may be transmitted because of intercourse. It explains such things as bleeding in pregnancy, miscarriage, contractions that are painless and some that are painful, and it gives good anecdotal accounts of labour.

So the title does not tell the reader about everything that is in this book. The book really is most valuable for all pregnant women to read whether they are wondering just about sex or about many other things. There is a particularly relevant section on contraception because fear of another pregnancy too soon after a baby has been born sometimes spoils the sex life of a couple, and Sylvia Close shows how to overcome that fear.

There is another particularly valuable chapter on the variations in menstruation, and another one about the variations in the degrees of sexual desire, not only during pregnancy but after childbirth. One of the most common complaints that couples have is that the woman has 'gone off' sex after the birth of the baby.

Sylvia Close poses all the questions and where answers are known she gives those answers.

I am very glad to have been able to have the chance of reading this book before it was published and can recommend it as a superb guide to all those in a partnership or a marriage who have questions that they are ashamed to ask.

ELLIOT PHILIPP M.A., M.B., B.Ch., F.R.C.S., F.R.C.O.G.
Consultant Obstetrician and Gynaecologist

Introduction

The need for this book was brought home to me during many years of work as an antenatal teacher. Pregnancy and the period immediately after childbirth pose special problems and engender specific anxieties in a sexual relationship. This became evident from the questions that cropped up again and again in the classes. Invariably someone would be concerned about harm to the baby or jeopardy to the pregnancy from sexual intercourse. Often the girl would say that it was her partner who was worried about the matter. On one occasion it led to the realization by a girl, who was then six months pregnant, that there had been no need for her and her husband to have abstained from intercourse from the time her pregnancy was confirmed.

Loss of sexual interest (which occasionally happens) quite naturally resulted in understandable anxiety and there was obvious relief to know that it was only a temporary state and that others had been similarly affected. Those who had genital infections worried about the effect on the baby – by either the infection or the medication. Some wanted to know about the venereal diseases.

There was generally a desire for information about miscarriage and premature labour. And many wanted to understand things that happened to friends – for example: how could someone who had had a child become infertile? Was it because her husband had become impotent?

Towards the end of the pregnancy the women tended to think ahead and their interest progressed to the re-establishment of menstruation and fertility, contraception, and whether it was possible to choose the sex of the next baby.

There were those who were too shy to broach their particular problem in class and they would stay behind to discuss it privately. Others felt more able to communicate by phone. Occasionally the problem or anxiety related to a sexual practice which was unusual and they needed to talk about it.

A feature of the antenatal course was the 'fathers' evening'. It was really meant to give husbands an understanding of the labour process and guidelines for helping their wives in labour. The discussion period, however, often brought forth questions about sex. Many men wanted to know how soon after the birth intercourse could be resumed and some were genuinely worried about vaginal distension during childbirth and whether the vagina would ever return to normal. Once they understood the physiology involved and how it can be aided, they were greatly reassured.

Sex can help to bond a couple and cement a relationship. To this end it is important that sexual anxieties and problems be resolved so that both partners may enjoy confidence and peace of mind.

I hope that this book – set out in the question and answer format for easy reference – will be found helpful by couples at this very special time in their lives.

Part 1 During Pregnancy

Are there times during pregnancy when intercourse should be avoided?

Until quite recently couples were advised to abstain from intercourse for the first three months of the pregnancy. The reason given was that the placenta was not yet sufficiently formed to anchor the foetus firmly and that intercourse could trigger off a miscarriage. The times when the menstrual periods would have been due were thought to be particularly hazardous. This posed a great problem for women with irregular cycles and those who were vague about the date of the last period. They either abstained or felt anxious and guilty if they did have intercourse. Abstinence was also advocated in the last two (and sometimes even three) months of the pregnancy with the object of preventing a premature birth and/or possible infections.

Since then, various research studies have established that the act of intercourse itself cannot jeopardize a *normal* pregnancy and cause a miscarriage or a premature labour. If love-making could terminate a pregnancy so easily then it would be a simple way of avoiding unwanted babies!

As for infection, this seems an unlikely hazard in a monogamous relationship. If, however, either of the couple has other sex partners then there is a possible risk of a sexually-transmitted infection. The danger is not intercourse itself but the genital health of casual sex partners. Nor can intercourse infect a baby who is well protected inside an intact bag of waters, inside the uterus. There is no open channel between the vagina and the developing foetus. The only way the baby can be infected during intra-uterine life is through the placental circulation, and then only if the mother is infected with certain blood-borne organisms that can pass through the placenta to the baby (see p.38).

Today it is accepted that couples can have intercourse safely from the onset of the pregnancy until virtually the beginning of labour, provided that:

1. The pregnancy is progressing normally and there are no contra-indications such as vaginal bleeding or 'spotting' (slight stainings of blood), and/or abnormal abdominal cramping.

2. The woman has no history of miscarriage or premature birth, and equally important,

3. The couple wish it.

Confidence that intercourse cannot harm the pregnancy is of the utmost importance for relaxed and enjoyable sexual relationships as the following example illustrates:

> During my second pregnancy everything was much better because I knew much more about the whole process and was confident that . . . the baby could not be harmed by intercourse, and that we might as well enjoy our undisturbed nights as long as we could!

If there are any contra-indications, the doctor should give definite guidance (preferably to both partners) about intercourse: when to abstain, for how long and the reason for the ban. If such advice has not been given, then do ask your doctor direct questions about intercourse and do not just skirt around the subject and expect him to guess what is on your mind. Also, do not let embarrassment prevent you from being quite clear about the details of whatever advice he does give you, otherwise you will merely be confused – as happened in this case:

> I had a threatened miscarriage at fourteen weeks and my doctor advised us to be careful during intercourse and not penetrate too deeply. This left me confused and worried as I didn't know what 'careful' meant and was terrified of losing the baby – which didn't make for the happiest love-life!

Is the abdominal cramping associated with orgasm harmful to mother or baby?

When a woman has an orgasm, it is thought that the hormone oxytocin is released from her pituitary gland. This hormone is also released during labour and, as in labour, oxytocin causes the uterus to contract, so the cramping felt either during or after an orgasm is due to this involuntary contraction of the uterus.

As to any associated dangers – none are known. What is known is that during these contractions the blood supply to the placenta, and therefore to the baby, is slightly reduced, causing the baby's heart to slow down a little. But this does the baby no harm at all and the heartbeat returns to normal very quickly afterwards. The same process occurs throughout labour without harming the baby, even if the labour lasts as long as 24 hours (which is considered normal for a first labour).

As far as the mother is concerned, the uterus normally contracts intermittently throughout the pregnancy and right up to the end of it. These painless Braxton-Hicks contractions cause no harm and women are not even aware of them. No doubt the uterus contracts more strongly when there is a sudden increased release of oxytocin but the effect is short-lived and not enough to set off labour – except possibly at full term when the cervix is 'ripe' and by which time the onset of labour will be welcomed.

Most women are quite unaware of any uterine contractions associated with orgasm, others are only mildly aware of the cramping low down in the abdomen, but some find the cramping so uncomfortable that they actually avoid orgasms when pregnant – as in the following instance:

At the beginning of my pregnancy I was a little wary of making love as it had taken us several years to conceive a baby. My fears, however, were based more on the thought of my husband's penetration rather than any consideration about an orgasm causing a miscarriage.

In a non-pregnant state I have always had quite intense orgasms and have been very aware of the rhythmic movements of the vagina. In pregnancy they were if anything more intense and just as enjoyable.

It was when I was about sixteen weeks pregnant that I was a little frightened. The orgasm seemed normal and enjoyable and then suddenly I was aware of my uterus in the form of a solid little ball and although it wasn't painful, it was extremely uncomfortable. What was rather disconcerting too, was the fact that no matter how I tried to relax the muscles, the area remained very hard. I went to sleep soon after this and was relieved to find everything normal in the morning.

I naturally read what articles I could find on the subject and all were reassuring, though vague.

We continued to make love quite regularly but I refrained from reaching a climax myself except when I felt a real desire. The funny thing was, as soon as I'd decided to abstain I felt a greater desire to reach a climax.

As my uterus grew in size I noticed the 'hardening' happening gradually as I became sexually aroused. I stopped reaching a climax altogether after an occasion when I was seven months pregnant. The uterus not only went very hard at the time, but it seemed irritated and sensitive for days afterwards. Everytime I touched my abdomen, every time I even thought about it, my uterus would go 'solid' and very uncomfortable.

In spite of all the cramping this woman experienced with love-making during her pregnancy, she had a perfectly normal healthy baby.

Which sexual practices should be avoided during pregnancy?

There are only a few practices which should be avoided during pregnancy. An obvious example is to avoid heavy, direct pressure (such as the man's weight) on the enlarging pregnant uterus when making love.

A problem which affects some women is that they just cannot lie on their backs in the latter months of pregnancy. If they do, their blood-pressure drops alarmingly. This makes them feel faint, they come out in a sweat and look pale. This condition is known as the 'supine hypotensive syndrome' and is caused by the pregnant uterus compressing the large blood vessel (inferior vena cava) and thus restricting the blood flow from the lower part of the body to the heart. If the woman turns onto the left side, this will alleviate all the symptoms and make her feel better almost immediately.

It therefore helps if the couple experiment in early pregnancy (if they have not already done so previously) with various new positions for intercourse so that as the pregnancy advances, they can adjust more easily and adopt positions for love-making other than the missionary one (i.e. face to face and with the man on top).

If intercourse has been vetoed for good reason, then masturbation to orgasm should also be avoided. This is because it is thought that orgasms resulting from masturbation tend to be more intense than orgasms from intercourse and the associated uterine contractions therefore also tend to be much stronger.

Even though a woman may be advised to avoid orgasm, the couple can and should learn ways of caressing and loving which will suit both of them while the ban lasts. In this way they can maintain and perhaps even strengthen the bond between them.

Oral sex by itself is physiologically harmless, but in their search for variation couples can sometimes inadvertently introduce the dangerous practice of blowing air into the vagina.

Blown air is air under pressure and can be forced into the uterus, through the uterine lining and into the bloodstream. An air bubble in the bloodstream is known as an embolus.

An air embolus in the circulation can block a blood vessel and so obstruct the blood supply to a vital organ, e.g. the brain (cerebral embolism). It is a serious condition and can even result in sudden death.

For the same reason douching should also be avoided during pregnancy, as forceful douching (water under pressure) can result in either an air embolus or a fluid embolus, which is just as dangerous.

Does pregnancy affect a woman's interest in sex?

Many women go through pregnancy with no obvious change in their sexual feelings and desires. The following comment is fairly typical:

> I never went off sex during pregnancy; in a way there was something extra special about it. In the early stages I think we made love rather less frequently than usual. I tended to be a bit tired, and I suppose at the back of my mind was a bit of anxiety about the risk of miscarriage, although I knew there were no real grounds for this concern. Thereafter we carried on pretty much as normal.

However, some women do experience considerable variation in sexual desire. Emotional factors are mainly responsible for such change. Hormones are only an indirect cause – they just create the physical symptoms which make the woman sexually apathetic.

In early pregnancy, sexual interest can easily be dissipated by any of the following factors:

1. Some of the early physical symptoms of the pregnancy, such as sleepiness, nausea or the unaccustomed tenderness and enlargement of the breasts.

2. Fear of miscarriage – especially if a previous pregnancy has ended unsuccessfully.

   When I was pregnant with my second baby both I and my husband were interested but cautious as (a) we had already lost one baby at birth and (b) I had threatened to miscarry. We were advised to abstain for the first three months but still felt a little restrained even when the all clear was given.

3. A desire to 'guard' the pregnancy, which can be the result of difficulty in conceiving, as in the following case:

   I asked about intercourse as my husband and I had abstained from the week I was overdue. I told him (the doctor) intercourse worried me and that we had not had intercourse for six weeks. I was told if it worries you, don't, until you're twelve weeks pregnant. My husband and I did not have intercourse until I was sixteen weeks pregnant. We'd forgotten what it was like . . . My husband and I went through a bad patch. It had been sixteen weeks since we had intercourse. I was blamed as he (my husband) did not believe it was on medical advice that we should not indulge. I gave in. Needless to say, it did not bring on a miscarriage.

4. If love-making has not previously been satisfactory for the woman, then the pregnancy is a good excuse to avoid a repetition of disappointment.

5. If the woman does not love her partner, but only wants a baby,

then once she has conceived, she is no longer interested in making love.

6. A combination of factors:

> I must confess that I also felt disinclined to make love when pregnant though this was influenced by a fear of hurting the baby and also slight shame of my changing shape – completely irrational, I know, but I never felt very lovely when pregnant.

There are, on the other hand, women who actually experience heightened sexuality when they become pregnant. This may well be due to release from anxiety about either wanting to become pregnant or not wanting to become pregnant. Once the pregnancy is a fact, the woman accepts it, relaxes emotionally and so no longer inhibits her feelings and reactions:

> When I was pregnant with my first baby I found I was more interested in making love because I felt more relaxed.

In mid-pregnancy, the time when most women feel at their best, sexual interest tends to revert to normal (if it had been affected in early pregnancy) or may even be increased.

In late pregnancy, women's interest in sex is again likely to vary. Some women lose interest because they are afraid of hurting the baby or of initiating a premature labour, or because intercourse becomes physically uncomfortable:

> I must admit that it all became a bit trying during the last month – uncomfortable because of my size and despite lubrication, rather painful. I'm looking forward to a rapid return to normal!

However, many women continue to be sexually active right up until the end of the pregnancy:

> My husband and I continued sexual relations until I was just over eight months pregnant and I would add that I found I seemed to enjoy it more as well and to feel the need for intimacy more frequently.

But the exact opposite also occurs:

> I was not interested in making love throughout the nine
> months and in fact towards the end, the very thought made
> me shudder!

And some develop bouts of heightened sexuality:

> I went through a period which lasted about three months
> when I wasn't really interested in love-making at all. Then in
> the last month, when I felt the least attractive, I suddenly
> turned into a raving sex maniac. I couldn't leave my husband
> alone.

So sexual interest during pregnancy does vary considerably and
tends to depend on the individual woman and her circumstances,
as well as on the stage of pregnancy.

Does pregnancy affect the man's interest in sex?

A man is obviously not himself affected physiologically or
hormonally by his partner's pregnancy, hence there are no *physical*
reasons for any change in his sexual appetite. Most men, however,
are affected *emotionally* and their attitude to intercourse with the
pregnant partner can vary almost as much as the reaction of
pregnant women themselves – though, of course, the reaction of
the man and the woman is not necessarily the same, and this may
therefore result in a slight conflict which needs understanding,
consideration and a little 'give and take' from each partner:

> My husband's attitude to me while I feel disinterested in sex
> is most sympathetic and we get by on a very basic shallow
> level, quite secure in the knowledge that it is only a passing
> phase.

Women often fear that as the pregnancy advances, their changing figure makes them look unattractive and even grotesque and will affect their partner's sexual interest in them. Although this does apply to a small minority, on the whole, many men tend to find the pregnant figure sexually stimulating:

My husband does not think pregnant women are beautiful and although he did his best to boost my ego, I knew what he really thought. It was, however, very interesting to see other men's reactions to a pregnant woman. Four of my husband's friends had a real infatuation for women in this condition and would immediately want to give me a cuddle and touch my stomach – delighting if the baby moved. Both my husband and I found the intensity of these feelings rather embarrassing – especially him as he used to feel most peculiar if the baby moved violently inside the womb.

Many men are proud to be responsible for the woman's pregnant state and tend to be particularly loving as the pregnancy advances. Women, however, will only be reassured about this if they are actually told so:

My husband was quite happy about having intercourse during pregnancy and I felt that I was being over-cautious. He tells me that he thinks that women are especially attractive when pregnant, so I did feel attractive myself.

It is probably true to say that on the whole men tend to take their cue from the woman and will be affected by her reaction to the pregnancy. For example, if the couple have planned the pregnancy and the woman is happy, well and eager for sexual encounters, then the man's sexual interest in her is likely to increase and he will be happy to continue intercourse and love-making while she desires it. If, on the other hand, the woman cheated and the pregnancy was not planned and the man neither wants nor is ready for fatherhood and feels trapped, then his anger and resentment is likely to be less conducive to love-making. This sort of situation may even push him to seek sexual partners outside the relationship.

A man is also likely to be affected by the woman's early physical changes such as sleepiness, nausea or anxiety about miscarriage. These and similar changes may act as a turn-off for him.

In most relationships there is one partner who is a little more anxious than the other and this can apply to the 'guarding' of the pregnancy, when it is often the man, rather than the woman, who is over-anxious, and fearful of dislodging the foetus:

> As I began to grow my husband expressed what is probably a very natural concern of a father not to hurt the baby, but again was reassured that the baby was quite safe. We noticed, incidentally, that the baby never moved around while we were making love: very well-behaved!

Occasionally a man will opt for complete abstinence during the pregnancy. He seems to be quite happy and content with close-togetherness, cuddling and alternative forms of love-making. (Pregnancy is of course a good time for experimenting and finding new ways of showing tenderness and expressions of love.) It is not always clear what the reason is for such a choice: he may be sensitive to and responding to his partner's feelings on the matter; he may feel his responsibility as protector of mother, foetus and pregnancy too keenly; he may be strongly motivated by religion or other cultural attitudes; or for him pregnancy may be a sexual turn-off.

A few women tend to become very introspective and obsessed with the pregnancy and the baby to the exclusion of everything else – including the baby's father. This situation is upsetting for the man who feels rejected and shut-out and women should guard against such complete involvement if they want to avoid the possibility of a rift in the relationship.

Rather surprisingly, in the latter part of the pregnancy, some men become sexually inhibited because they feel that there is a 'third person' present who is observing and judging their performance. Others fear that the penis will hurt the baby's head, and one man jokingly used to tell the baby to 'duck' when he and his wife had intercourse.

To summarise: it is impossible to predict how an individual man will react but, in general, the happier and more positive the woman is about her pregnancy, the more likely it is that her partner will react similarly. Such a positive situation augers well for a sexually happy pregnancy for both partners. Each partner affects the other, and each one needs reassurance, tenderness and love.

What causes a miscarriage?

It is not always possible to know the exact reason for a miscarriage without careful examination of the expelled products and other investigations. There are many possible causes but the more usual ones are due to either the foetus itself or the foetal environment.

Foetal causes

1. An imperfect embryo resulting from some defect of either the egg or the sperm, or failure of the fertilized egg to develop normally.

2. A less common cause is a drug-damaged embryo or a virus-damaged embryo. In early pregnancy many drugs, as well as some virus infections of the mother, may harm the developing foetus and result in failure of either embryo or placenta to develop normally.

Environmental factors

These may result in faulty implantation of the embryo in the uterus and may be due to:

1. Some abnormality of the uterus, e.g. a double uterus (this is a rare condition).

2. Uterine fibroids which distort the cavity of the uterus and limit the area suitable for implantation and growth of the foetus.

3. Hormonal deficiency, i.e. insufficient ovarian hormones to tide the pregnancy over until the placenta is formed and starts to produce an adequate amount of the essential hormones:

   I conceived my first baby quickly, carried her easily and led a normal life right up to her birth. Then I had three heart-breaking miscarriages – at six, eight and thirteen weeks – the last one accompanied by a haemorrhage and ending with a blood transfusion... When I began to bleed the next time at seven weeks, I was given a test for the progesterone content of the cervical mucus. As a result I was given injections of progesterone . . . When I had had the treatment for eight weeks the pregnancy was securely anchored, the progesterone stopped and a lovely little girl arrived at full term. She's now six months old and at her assessment was pronounced 'perfect'.

   This treatment is controversial and many doctors prefer to treat cases of habitual abortion differently.

4. Nutritional deficiency. If the mother is malnourished then she lacks an adequate store of nutrients for the normal development of the foetus. A deficiency of folic acid (one of the B vitamins) is known to result in miscarriage. This is why a folic-acid supplement is given almost routinely to all pregnant women. Insufficient vitamin E may be another factor responsible for a miscarriage. At one antenatal clinic where I worked, women who had had two or three successive miscarriages were given vitamin E from early in the next pregnancy with very good results. No doubt there are other nutrients, as yet not identified, which are essential for the healthy growth of the developing embryo.

5. An 'incompetent cervix' due to some previous injury to the

cervix. In such cases, half way through the pregnancy, when the foetus gets big enough and distends the cavity of the uterus, the damaged cervix opens and a miscarriage follows. This is easily prevented in a subsequent pregnancy by having a 'purse-string' stitch inserted around the cervix to keep it closed. It is known as a Shirodkar Suture and is removed about two weeks before full term.

6. Emotional factors. Miscarriages have been known to occur after shock, grief or some other severe emotional stress. Emotions do affect the body's internal functioning and it may be that in cases of severe shock, the associated sudden lowering of the mother's blood-pressure lessens the circulation of blood to the uterus. The embryo is deprived of oxygen and dies. The uterus will then expel it as a miscarriage. There may, therefore, be some validity in the old wives' tale that a pregnant woman should be cossetted and protected from distressing news, situations and sights in order to preserve her emotional equilibrium and not jeopardize the pregnancy through emotional distress.

Warning signs

The two signs of threatened miscarriage are bleeding and abdominal cramp. Although bleeding is more frightening for the woman, it may in fact be less serious than the cramps. The bleeding may be due to hormonal imbalance which may right itself, or it may be caused by the embryo becoming slightly loosened from the uterine wall and this, too, may settle down. The cramps, however, are in fact contractions of the uterus which dilate the cervix and try to expel what is inside. At the first indication of either of these symptoms, the woman should be under the care of her doctor until the condition is resolved one way or the other. If a miscarriage does occur, what comes away should, if possible, be kept for the doctor to examine.

Ectopic pregnancies

Women also need to know that a less common but more serious way of losing a pregnancy is if the fertilized egg fails to reach the uterus. Fertilization of the egg by the sperm takes place in the fallopian tube (the two fallopian tubes begin on either side of the upper part of the uterus and lead to the ovaries). Once fertilized, the egg grows by cell division. At the same time it is propelled along by the undulating movement of the cilia (little hairs) in the fallopian tube to the uterus, where a special new lining has developed to support and feed the growing embryo.

Very occasionally, because of some abnormality of the tube – either a narrowing (often caused by a previous infection) or malfunctioning – the fertilized egg cannot get into the uterus and continues to grow in the fallopian tube. Unlike the uterus which can accommodate two, three or more babies if necessary, the tube cannot stretch in the same way and is soon strained to its full capacity. It then bursts, there is internal bleeding and the embryo falls into the pelvic cavity and dies. This is known as a 'ruptured ectopic'. (It has been known for the embryo to attach itself to the contents in the pelvis and continue to grow to full term, but this is very rare.)

It may not be easy for a midwife or doctor to diagnose an ectopic pregnancy but there should be no mistaking a ruptured ectopic. The signs are severe low abdominal pain, vaginal bleeding which may be slight as most of the bleeding is internal, and some degree of shock. The woman is pale and looks ill; she feels faint and nauseous. This condition is an emergency and medical help should be urgently sought.

For the woman who wants a baby, a miscarriage is the death of a hope. The people around her should be sensitive to this and not only give her their sympathy but also time and opportunity to get over her bitter disappointment.

If intercourse is painful should it be avoided?

The state of pregnancy does not in itself cause intercourse to be painful, so abstaining will not solve a problem which may therefore persist and still be there after the baby is born. Instead, the actual cause of the discomfort needs to be identified and dealt with. There are many factors which can be responsible for uncomfortable or even painful intercourse. Some are simple and easily corrected; others require medical help.

Possible causes of discomfort for women

One obvious cause of mild but off-putting discomfort is a full bladder.

Lack of lubrication
Another frequent cause is lack of the natural lubricant which is exuded from the walls of the vagina when a woman is sexually aroused. Any anxiety or fear related to the pregnancy, fatigue, or general sexual apathy will inhibit vaginal lubrication. In addition to tackling the emotional aspect (which is highly individual and will therefore vary from woman to woman), a practical way of overcoming the physical aspect of this problem is to use a non-irritating and non-greasy lubricating jelly or cream. An even simpler alternative is saliva, which is quite an adequate lubricant for the odd occasion.

There will, of course, also be discomfort from lack of lubrication if a woman accepts penetration before she is ready for it. In this instance what is needed is honest verbal communication between the woman and her partner. Women vary considerably in their response to stimulation and a couple should get to know each other's sexual needs and preferences fairly early in a relationship so that positive techniques can be reinforced to give both partners pleasure. If not, the negative aspects are perpetuated, leading to resentment, frustration and unhappiness for the woman. Shyness can be a great communication barrier and if initially a woman finds it difficult to talk about her needs, then during love-making she can gently guide her partner's hand either to make the wanted stimulation or to stop some irritating gesture. For example, a caress can be off-putting if done too quickly or too hard; if done too lightly, it can tickle and irritate; if done slowly and with just the right pressure, it can be sexually exciting.

Love-making positions

A woman may find that pressure on her abdomen – especially in the second half of the pregnancy – is uncomfortable and detracts from enjoyment. This may be misinterpreted as painful intercourse. Changing love-making positions will solve this problem. Alternatively, pressure on the abdomen can be avoided if the man supports his weight on his hands. This is how one couple, who were expecting twins, solved their particular problem, as the woman was only comfortable when lying on her back.

Vaginal irritation

Vaginal irritation, inflammation or infection, due to a variety of causes (see Infections, p.29), can make intercourse uncomfortable or painful. Daily gentle washing of the area with lukewarm water and a mild non-irritating soap is the first step in dealing with the problem, but too frequent washing and cleansing will make the tissues even more sensitive. Avoid harsh soaps, vaginal deodorants, perfumed toiletries to which you may be allergic, internal tampons (to absorb vaginal discharge) and other likely irritants. If at all possible wear cotton rather than nylon underwear and make sure that it is not too tight as both nylon and the close fit of the pants will help to keep the moisture in, the air out, will irritate the tissues and so aggravate the condition. Frequent cold water splashing can soothe the inflamed area, relieve any itching and reduce the temptation to scratch. Scratching should be avoided as it will further damage the tissues, prevent healing and there is also the risk of introducing a secondary infection. Even if itching is the only symptom you have, do not ignore it if it persists, as it can sometimes be due to sugar in the urine and may require further investigation.

One surprising but effective soothing and healing agent is

natural unsweetened yogurt which can help to restore the vagina to its normal healthy state. The yogurt has to be applied directly to the inflamed vaginal tissues several times a day. It probably also helps to *eat* a fair amount of the natural unsweetened yogurt as it helps to restore the normal bowel bacteria and will therefore create an unfavourable environment for organisms which might have been introduced from the bowel and were the original cause of the vaginal infection (see p.43). The yogurt treatment is worth trying for at least a week. If there is no improvement, seek medical help. Your doctor can then diagnose the cause of the vaginal discomfort and prescribe specific treatment.

Varicose veins
During pregnancy there is increased congestion in the pelvic area. Some women even have varicose veins in the vulva or vagina, and may find that the added congestion associated with sexual arousal will give rise to discomfort or pain. Resting for about ten minutes with the hips raised, and applying cold compresses to the varicose veins, can reduce the congestion quite considerably and is worth doing before making love (as well as at other times for increased comfort).

Gynaecological problems
Other possible causes of pain during love-making might be conditions such as fibroids, ovarian cysts, inflammation of the fallopian tubes and other gynaecological problems which are unrelated to the pregnancy itself. Avoiding deep penile penetration or changing love-making positions may help to prevent pain from such causes. But again, your doctor should diagnose the cause and advise you about treatment which, on occasion, may even have to be delayed until after the baby is born.

These are the most common physical causes for uncomfortable or painful intercourse and there is no need either to 'submit and suffer in silence' or to avoid love-making completely. Working together, a couple can overcome most difficulties and in doing so they strengthen their relationship.

Possible causes of discomfort for men

Men, too, can experience painful intercourse. One obvious cause is a foreskin which is too tight (phimosis). The foreskin cannot easily be retracted over the penile glans and this causes pressure and pain on erection, penetration and thrusting. Also, since the foreskin cannot easily be retracted, the secretions (smegma) underneath accumulate and cause irritation and inflammation. (This can also happen with a normal foreskin if hygiene is poor.)

Acute sensitivity or allergy may result in itching, inflammation or blistering of the penis. The allergen can be a particular brand of lubricant used, or any one of the partner's toiletries.

Vaginal infections can spread to the penis causing burning, itching and acute discomfort. If the penile urethra is involved and becomes inflamed, then severe pain can be experienced when ejaculating.

A temporary side-effect of some drugs, which tend to dry up secretions in the body, may be to cause the semen to become too viscid. This, too, results in painful ejaculation. In later life, an inflamed or enlarged prostate gland is another reason for painful ejaculation.

Help for all these conditions should be sought early as they are all medically (or surgically) treatable.

What are the various genital or vaginal infections and can they harm the baby?

The genital tract is normally kept moist and comfortable by an exudation or secretion from the cervix and vaginal walls. This exudation is clear, colourless, mucousy in consistency (similar to white of egg or saliva) and quite inoffensive in smell. During pregnancy there is an increase in these secretions and it is therefore quite normal to have a slight discharge from the vagina. (This also happens during ovulation and sexual arousal.)

Any discharge which is profuse, or purulent (pus-like) or frothy, or yellow, red, brown, black, or greenish in colour, or has an offensive smell, or irritates and inflames the tissues making them red, raw and swollen, or causes itching or scratching is abnormal. It is an indication of an infection or an allergic irritation of the vagina or cervix, and needs investigation by a doctor. (It is also worth knowing that a discharge can result from frequent douching or douching with irritating substances.)

The organisms causing the infection may be bacterial, viral, fungal, or parasitic in origin. Many are sexually transmitted (the so-called 'venereal diseases') and it is even possible to have more than one infection at the same time.

A few of the organisms may be present in a woman's genital tract, in a dormant state, for long periods – even years – without causing any symptoms at all. They will only become active and troublesome if the environment becomes favourable for them. This is likely to happen:

1. When a woman is run-down or generally below par.

2. After taking a course of antibiotics which destroy not only the harmful germs in the body but also the normal vaginal bacteria, thus making conditions suitable for other organisms to flourish.

3. If the contraceptive pill is taken, as it alters the normal vaginal environment.

4. As a result of douching, e.g. an alkaline douche will not only neutralize the normal acid vaginal environment and adversely affect the vaginal flora but will actually predispose to infections.

Some of these infections, although distressingly unpleasant, are mainly a nuisance and with the right treatment will clear up quickly and without complications or danger to the baby. Other infections, however, do involve risk of serious complications as well as dangers for the baby.

Monilia (vaginal thrush)

One of the less damaging but nevertheless annoying infections is *monilia* (also known as vaginal thrush) which is caused by a fungus *(candida albicans)*. Many women unknowingly harbour the fungus in the vagina or bowel, but it only becomes active and flourishes when conditions become favourable. Pregnancy favours the proliferation of the fungus for several reasons. One is that the fungus loves warmth and moisture and the increased blood supply and increased secretions makes the vagina an ideal habitat. Other favourable conditions are the higher oestrogen level and the higher glycogen content of the vaginal tissues. Attacks or flare-ups of vaginal thrush are therefore fairly common during pregnancy.

The monilia discharge is thick, white, curd-like and very irritating. The infection does not threaten the pregnancy, nor can it harm the baby before birth. But it should be treated and cleared up before labour starts, otherwise the baby is likely to be infected with the fungus as he/she comes down the birth canal and may later suffer from thrush in the mouth. (Should this happen, it can easily be cured.)

Monilia in men does not present itself in the same way as in women. Conditions, on the whole, are not favourable for growth of the fungus on the male genitals. Men, however, can and do harbour the fungus in various parts of the body such as under the foreskin and in the alimentary tract, which stretches from the mouth to the anus, and the penis can be irritated by the partner's vaginal discharge during intercourse. So the man, too, should be treated, otherwise he is likely to reinfect the woman again and again:

My first bout of thrush occurred after a course of antibiotics. There was then a gap of two years before the next bout. Both of these were cleared up with . . . pessaries and cream. I have suffered with an infertility problem for some five years. . . . During this period of time thrush reared its ugly head again not just once but every month, seven to ten days before my period when apparently the hormone levels change, and because I was being treated with hormone fertility drugs this made me more susceptible to thrush. Of course when one has thrush you have to avoid sexual contact with your partner as it can 'ping-pong' backwards and forwards[1] and having this every month certainly did not help with my fertility problem.

I ate natural yogurt,[2] which I have been told helps, and wore open-gusset tights and cotton underwear as thrush loves a warm moist atmosphere which is created by nylon.

Even though my husband has never had any symptoms of thrush the doctor told me to make sure he was treated with cream each time I had thrush as he could re-infect me and I would never be clear of it.

Trichomonas

Another fairly common infestation during pregnancy is trichomonas. This is caused by a tiny one-celled protozoa parasite which is mostly active during a woman's reproductive years, i.e. from puberty to the menopause. The parasite can, however, inhabit the vagina and sometimes even the bladder or urethra for years without causing any troublesome symptoms. Unlike the monilia fungus, the trichomonas parasite does not live in the alimentary tract.

The trichomonas discharge is profuse, frothy, causes severe itching and irritation, is foul-smelling and yellow or greenish in colour. The condition does not threaten the pregnancy and there is no risk of miscarriage, nor can the parasite affect a woman's future fertility.

[1] Not all doctors advise abstaining from intercourse during an attack of monilia because both partners should be getting treatment and it is a good way of giving the man a dose of the anti-fungal cream if he is not being treated.

[2] In addition to eating yogurt, it should also be inserted into the vagina where it is thought to help normalize the environment and destroy pathogenic organisms.

Although a trichomonas infection usually causes a vaginitis (inflammation of the vagina), it can also cause a urethritis (inflammation of the urethra).

As the parasite likes a moist environment, a good precautionary measure is to be fastidious about such things as other people's damp towels, damp face flannels, damp bathing suits, and even droplets on lavatory seats, as it is thought that all these may be a source of infection, although mainly it is sexually transmitted. Good genital hygiene may be a way of keeping the parasite inactive and possibly even destroying it, as it does not like soap. (Conditions favourable for trichomonas are also favourable for the organism that causes the more serious disease gonorrhoea, and it is possible to have both infections at the same time.)

Men can harbour the parasite in the genito-urinary tract and under the foreskin without having any untoward symptoms at all. In some, however, the parasite becomes active and causes a urethritis with a discharge, and an itch at the tip of the penis. The infection may disappear spontaneously after a few weeks.

Treatment, when prescribed, should be for both partners, even if the man shows no signs of infestation. Should the woman have an attack of trichomonas early in pregnancy (i.e. in the first twelve to fourteen weeks) then it is important that her doctor knows that she is pregnant or likely to be pregnant because some authorities do not consider the medicine which is specific for trichomonas to be safe during pregnancy or while the woman is breast-feeding.

Genital warts

One of the effects of today's greater sexual freedom is an increase in sexually-transmitted infections. One such infection is genital warts. These are caused by a virus and are very contagious. The most common site is around the vagina and anus, but they have also been known to develop inside the vagina and on the cervix. Warts, too, need warmth and moisture for growth and the extra secretions of pregnancy make it a favourable time for them to appear. They are also likely to be found in women who have a chronic vaginal discharge or who have increased vaginal secretions during pregnancy or while taking the contraceptive pill. Without treatment, and if conditions are favourable, warts can proliferate to an alarming degree and have even been known to block the vaginal opening.

The warts are itchy and irritating, and scratching not only helps them to spread but also risks a secondary infection.

As the warts are mostly localized around the external genitalia, they cannot affect the baby, but they should be removed and cleared before the women goes into labour.

In men the favourite site for warts is under the foreskin and on the glans of the penis. Less frequently, they may be found on the shaft of the penis.

Since warts are so highly contagious, treatment should be given to both partners at the same time. If your pregnancy has only just started, do tell your doctor that you are pregnant to ensure that you are not given medication which will harm the developing baby.

The condition has been known to improve spontaneously after the pregnancy when the warts may disappear completely.

Herpes

Another sexually-transmitted infection which is much more prevalent today than formerly is herpes of the genitals. This, too, is due to a viral infection. The offending virus may be either the relatively harmless one that causes 'cold sores' round the mouth and nose (Herpes Simplex Virus type I) which poses no threat to the baby, or it may be a related but more serious one (Herpes Simplex Virus type II). Although the two infections are similar, the latter is thought to be a precursor of cancer of the cervix. The general symptoms of the more serious genital herpes are similar to those of other virus infections such as 'flu: a rise in temperature, general malaise with loss of appetite, and swollen glands. In addition, the local symptoms are the herpes blisters which usually appear round the orifices in the body and where skin and mucous membrane meet – round the vagina, urethra and anus. But they may also develop inside the vagina and on the cervix, causing a discharge and vaginal spotting (very slight bleeding).

The blisters are painful and intensely itchy and the affected parts are inflamed and swollen. The blisters may rupture and develop into open sores with the added risk of becoming infected with another organism (i.e. a secondary infection). Then there is the added agony of painful urination if the urethral area is involved. As there is yet no specific drug available for a viral infection, some comfort and relief may be had from splashing cold water on the affected area which can help to reduce the swelling, inflammation and pain. It also helps to avoid extra pressure from tight underwear and tight trousers. (Again, be cautious about medication which could harm the baby.)

The blisters become pustules and burst before they dry and heal. The attack may take a few weeks to clear, and the virus then enters the latent stage when it is thought less likely to be contagious (but this has not been definitely proved).

Once a woman has had an attack of genital herpes, she is liable to recurrent bouts especially when she is below par in health or when subjected to physical or emotional stress. This is because the virus has not been completely destroyed and she still harbours it. Subsequent attacks tend to be less severe and less painful than the first.

An infection during pregnancy may result in a miscarriage, premature labour or stillbirth. If an attack of herpes occurs in early pregnancy and a miscarriage does not result, then it may possibly be worth considering a termination of the pregnancy as some viruses are thought to damage the tiny foetus in the first twelve to fourteen weeks of its development. Anyone who finds herself in such a situation should discuss this point with the doctors at the special clinic and should be guided by their advice and experience. If a woman has an attack towards the end of her pregnancy and it has not cleared by the time she is full term, then the obstetrician will probably decide to deliver the baby by Caesarean section as a precaution against infecting the baby when he/she passes down the birth canal. A newborn baby infected with the herpes virus is at risk of getting viral encephalitis (inflammation of the brain) which could be fatal.

Men, too, can get genital herpes and their symptoms are similar to those of their sexual partners.

Bacterial infections

These can be caused by any one of the many pathogenic bacteria. The discharge will vary according to the infection but is generally yellowish or greenish in colour. Bacterial infections respond well to treatment with antibiotics. An example of a less serious bacterial infection for the woman is *haemophilus vaginalis* which is characterized by a greyish discharge with an offensive smell. With the right treatment, the condition can be cleared within a week. Sexual partners, of course, need to be treated too.

Should the infection reach the baby it is much more serious as both he/she and the amniotic fluid can be infected. This can result in septicaemia (blood poisoning) and death of the foetus.

Gonorrhoea

Gonorrhoea is an extremely serious bacterial infection which is very prevalent today. The offending organism is the *gonococcus* which is transmitted from an infected partner during sexual intercourse and settles in the cervix, which is a more favourable alkaline environment for it. The incubation period can vary from a day or two up to three weeks (or even later) after contact, depending on the virulence of the infection. The discharge is purulent (pus-like) and greenish in colour. The infection may involve the urethra, causing additional frequent and painful urination. Should one of the Bartholin glands (near the entrance of the vagina) be infected, an abscess will form and may suppurate.

If untreated, the infection may spread to the fallopian tubes to cause a very painful inflammation (salpingitis) with the risk of permanent damage such as narrowing or blockage of the tubes, which in turn may become the cause of later infertility. Even more serious complications will occur if the gonococcus enters the general circulation and is carried throughout the body. Then it may affect the heart valves, the tendons and joints to cause an arthritis-like condition (known as 'young man's arthritis') and the membranes covering the brain, to cause a gonorrhoeal meningitis. This type of meningitis is more common during pregnancy but we do not yet know why.

Ironically, the gonococcus is a delicate organism and dies if dried out, or exposed to cold or heat or sunlight, or an acid medium (which is why it lodges in the cervix which has an alkaline secretion). It can be killed by most disinfectants.

A gonorrhoeal infection in early pregnancy may result in a spontaneous abortion. Infection after the first three months of pregnancy tends to be temporarily localized in the area below the uterus because the thick gelatinous cervical mucus plug acts as a barrier.

Should the infection be untreated when the baby is born, then his/her eyes are likely to be infected at the time of birth causing a gonorrhoeal ophthalmia. This is so damaging to the baby's delicate eyes that it may, if neglected, lead to blindness.

Small girls can develop a gonorrhoeal vulvovaginitis (inflammation of the vulva and vagina) through hand to body contact with an infected adult.

The two main symptoms of a gonorrhoeal infection in men are a burning sensation when urinating; and a continuous purulent greenish discharge from the penis.

Anyone who suspects they may have contracted a gonorrhoeal infection, should get help as soon as possible both for themself and their sexual partner because gonorrhoea can be completely cured if treated promptly. It is often advisable to go directly to a 'venereal disease' treatment clinic (also known either as a 'Special' clinic or the 'Department of Genito-Urinary Medicine' in any hospital) so that expert diagnosis and treatment can be obtained, if necessary, without any delay.

You should also know that it is sometimes possible for a woman to be infected without showing any obvious symptoms. If this is not recognized, then she becomes a carrier and is still able to infect her sex partners.

Syphilis
The most serious of all the sexually-transmitted infections is

syphilis. This is because the spirochete (cork-screw organism or bacterium) responsible, named *treponema pallidum*, after penetrating healthy mucous membrane or a crack in the skin, enters the circulation and becomes a blood-borne infection. Thus the infection, unless halted, can spread to virtually every system and organ in the body to cause permanent and destructive damage. It can affect the circulatory system, the heart, the nervous system, brain, bones, joints, eyes, nose etc. The incubation period varies enormously – anything from two weeks to three months – but symptoms have been known to occur earlier.

THE FOUR STAGES OF SYPHILIS: *The primary stage* is characterized by a small hard mass which ulcerates and is known as a chancre. It appears at the site of infection, has a depressed centre and thickened outer rim, is painless, non-itchy and slow to heal (it can take up to six weeks to heal completely). It is easily missed if the site of infection is the cervix or the wall of the vagina. It can, however, be on the lip, tongue, nipple, finger or vulva. The nearest lymphatic glands to the chancre swell in their effort to halt the invading treponemes. But, unless treated, it is a losing battle. A positive diagnosis can be made from the contents of the glands, or exudation at the base of the chancre. Blood tests will only become positive about a month after the chancre first appeared.

The secondary stage will follow if the disease has not been diagnosed and treated. By now the treponemes are in the bloodstream, still multiplying and circulating to every part of the body. This shows itself as a generalized infection with flu-like symptoms of pains and aches in the joints and limbs, a raised temperature, general malaise, headache, sore throat, laryngitis, swollen glands and 'snail-track' ulcers in the mouth and throat. There may be involvement of other organs, e.g. inflammation of the eyes, or liver (hepatitis), or even the membranes covering the brain (meningitis). There is also a characteristic rash which is most marked on chest and forearms. It appears about six weeks after the chancre heals and is coppery-reddish-brown in colour and *does not itch*. Syphilitic growths (condylomata) can appear on the vulva and round the anus. They are raised moist flat discs, slightly dented on top with a greyish exudate and with an offensive smell. These are highly contagious. By now blood tests will give a positive result and if treatment is given, the disease can be cured. If untreated, attacks can recur for several years.

The latent stage begins when symptoms of secondary syphilis no longer recur. This is the 'hidden' stage and can last a very long time – up to 20 years or even a whole lifetime. During this stage, syphilis can be diagnosed by positive blood tests and if treatment is started, the disease can still be halted. The latent stage is not infectious – except to the foetus if the woman is pregnant, because the treponemes in her blood pass through the placenta to infect her baby with syphilis.

The tertiary stage is also not infectious. It is the time when the ravages of the disease show up as ulcer-like lesions *(gumma* or *gummata)* anywhere in the body – particularly the heart, blood vessels, brain, nervous system, etc. The two main forms of tertiary syphilis are:

1. general paralysis of the insane (GPI), with delusions of grandeur;

2. locomotor ataxia, with loss of reflexes and co-ordination of voluntary movement and posture.

This stage is irreversible and may occur any time from five years to fifty years after the initial infection.

SYPHILIS AND THE UNBORN BABY. If a pregnant woman is infected with syphilis, her unborn baby is at great risk of being similarly infected. The route of infection is through the placenta and as the placenta is not fully formed in the first sixteen weeks, the foetus is relatively safe until then. If the mother receives treatment from the beginning of the pregnancy, the baby will be completely protected.

Without treatment, the placenta at first attempts to filter the treponemes to prevent them reaching the foetus and in the process itself becomes infected. Then the foetus is doubly at risk – from a diseased placenta which is inefficient in providing adequate nutrients, and from the onslaught of a virulent infection.

The outlook for the untreated syphilitic foetus is grim and it may be aborted after twenty weeks, born dead (macerated foetus) – either prematurely or at full term, born alive (either prematurely or at full term) but suffering from congenital syphilis, or born apparently healthy and show effects of syphilis later.

Congenital syphilis in the baby is the same as secondary syphilis in the adult. The treponemes are in his/her system and can damage all parts of his/her body. The baby, if born alive, is small, puny and unhealthy. He/she may have a skin rash (syphilitic pemphigus). The mucous membrane in the nose and mouth may be affected causing a nasal catarrh (syphilitic snuffles) and sores and cracks at the corners of the mouth. The liver and spleen may be enlarged and the baby may be jaundiced. If treatment is started immediately after birth, further damage can be prevented.

Without treatment, the treponemes continue to destroy the body. The eyes can be affected (interstitial kerititis) and cause either impaired vision or blindness. If the ears are affected, it will result in deafness. There may be painful swellings of the bones and the long bones of the legs can become deformed (sabre tibia). The nose bones may be destroyed, resulting in a 'saddle' nose. The permanent front teeth may be deformed (Hutchinson's teeth). And, of course, the brain and spinal cord are also liable to be affected.

Once damage has occurred, it is permanent and the child carries the signs of congenital syphilis into adulthood. Further damage, however, can be prevented if treatment is begun, no matter at what stage.

Treatment for syphilis is effective and the sooner the disease is diagnosed and treatment begun, the better the chances of complete cure both for the mother and the baby. Because of the serious nature of the disease, blood tests for syphilis are carried out routinely at the beginning of every pregnancy to eliminate the possibility of the disease being present, and to start treatment as soon as possible if the disease has been diagnosed. Infected contacts should, of course, also be treated.

Yaws

Another condition which gives a positive result to tests for syphilis is *yaws*, because the offending organism *(treponema pertenue)* is very similar to that of syphilis. Yaws is a tropical, non-venereal disease which is spread by flies and by direct close physical (not sexual) contact. The only problem is that in a pregnant woman (who may have been infected in childhood) it is virtually impossible to differentiate between syphilis and latent yaws. Although yaws does not threaten the life or welfare of the unborn baby, nevertheless, treatment for syphilis will be given to the mother as a precaution, and to ensure the baby's health.

Pubic lice and scabies

These two non-vaginal parasitic infestations were previously associated only with poverty and dirt, but today they are becoming commonplace because they, too, are transmitted through close body contact such as that involved in sexual intercourse. Both infestations cause intense itching of the skin and require medical treatment.

Is it possible to avoid or prevent these infections?

As these infections and infestations are mostly transmitted sexually, the only sure way of avoiding them is to abstain from any form of sexual contact with another person. But this is unrealistic and possibly the safest situation is a monogamous relationship in which neither partner strays. If, in addition, neither partner's body harbours the various organisms, such as the monilia fungus and the trichomonas protozoa, in a dormant state, then they are relatively safe.

But whether you have, or do not have, or do not want the 'ideal' situation described, there are several precautions that can be observed.

Diet

A healthy body is good protection against infections and infestations. Health to a large extent depends on how the body is nourished and although good nutrition is fundamental for good health, there is no need to become obsessive or neurotic about diet. Nutrition is a new and complex science and we are gradually learning about all the many nutrients which the body needs – not only the proteins, fats and carbohydrates but the many vitamins, minerals and trace elements, as well as their correct combination and interactions in health and disease.

For practical purposes, however, the basic principles behind a good diet can be summarized as follows:

1. A varied diet, rather than a limited one of a few favoured foods, is by far the easiest way of ensuring that the body is given all the available nutrients for good health.

2. Fresh foods are preferable to tinned, frozen or preserved ones.

3. Fruit and vegetables should be eaten raw as well as cooked, as nutrients are lost in the cooking water and vitamin C is destroyed by heat.

4. Wholefoods are preferable to processed or convenience foods, e.g. brown rice contains the B vitamins and polished rice does not, wholewheat bread is more nutritious than white bread, etc.

5. Foods with chemical additives, such as artificial flavouring, colouring and preservatives, should as far as possible be avoided. Not only are some people allergic to additives, but some of the chemicals, e.g. nitrites, are suspected of being carcinogenic (capable of causing cancer).

6. Cut down sugar to a minimum. Too much of it can cause tooth decay, increased weight and interfere with the absorption of minerals such as calcium.

Aim for these principles even if they cannot always be achieved. If, during pregnancy, you establish a pattern of healthy eating for yourself and your partner, then not only will both of you as well as the baby in the uterus be well nourished, but after the baby is born and from about four months of age, you can gradually and with confidence introduce your child to the same healthy diet.

Relaxation techniques

Another factor in good health is to avoid over-reacting emotionally. The fatigue that follows emotional stress or an emotional upset is often far greater than any reaction to physical exertion. Fatigue and exhaustion lower one's resistance to infections, so it helps to teach oneself to be emotionally calm and not to over-react. This is not as difficult as it may seem. Try the following technique: when in a situation which is likely to make you over-react, try instead to gently purse your lips and blow out slowly and smoothly (not jerkily) and continue to blow out until your lungs are virtually empty. Allow your lungs to fill easily (but do not take a huge breath or gasp) and again slowly blow out the air through your pursed lips. Repeat this pattern of breathing until you have calmed down and you are again in control of your emotions. A few deep sighs (or yawns) may also do the trick and help you to calm down. A third way is just to consciously slow down your breathing.

Hygiene

Being careful about hygiene is another important preventative measure. The monilia fungus and many bacteria live in the bowel without causing any problems, but when these same organisms are introduced into the vagina they can set off an attack of vaginal thrush or a bacterial vaginitis. If the organisms are introduced into the urethra, they will spread to the bladder and cause an attack of cystitis (inflammation of the bladder). These infections from the bowel can mostly be avoided if women are careful about cleaning their bottoms from 'front to back' and not with a hand between the legs – which would automatically result in a wipe from anus to vulva, with risk of contamination. If your baby is a little girl then do get into the habit of cleaning her bottom from front to back right from the very first time that you change her nappy. When she is able to sit up, make sure that she is never left to *sit* in a nappy full of faecal matter. When she is a toddler, teach her to clean herself correctly, wiping from 'front to back'.

Another way of infecting the vagina is if anal sex precedes normal intercourse. This method of infection can be avoided if the penis is carefully washed before vaginal penetration. It also helps if men always wash their hands before making love.

Lavatories harbour organisms so when using public lavatories it is wise to avoid sitting on the seat; alternatively, you can line the seat with toilet paper. Another precaution is to place toilet paper in the lavatory pan to prevent the water splashing up onto your vulva. Always wash your hands afterwards in case someone has contaminated the flushing handle with faecal matter. As already mentioned, the trichomonas parasite can be picked up from damp towels, damp articles of personal clothing and even from damp lavatory seats, so it pays to be fastidious and avoid using them.

Most organisms responsible for these afflictions need warmth and moisture to proliferate. An example, given earlier, is the gonococcus (the organism responsible for gonorrhoea) which is destroyed if it dries out or is exposed to cold. Adults are most unlikely to get gonorrhoea from a lavatory seat, but a little girl could be infected if, by sliding onto the lavatory seat, her vulva came in contact with a blob of gonorrhoeal discharge shortly after it was deposited there.[1]

The vulva is more likely to be healthy, cool and dry if air is allowed to circulate freely round it. This is why it is better to wear cotton rather than nylon underwear, and skirts and dresses rather than tight trousers. This does not mean that tight trousers are taboo, but as they help to create a warm and damp environment, it

---

[1] This possibility will probably be disputed by most doctors but when I worked in a hospital for infectious diseases quite a number of little girls from unhygienic tenements were admitted with gonorrhoea. They had not been sexually assaulted and investigations suggested that lavatory-seat infection was a likely cause as many people shared the lavatories.

is better to wear them occasionally rather than constantly.

The greatest risk, of course, is having intercourse with partners whose state of genital health is unknown to you. Under these circumstances it is better if the man uses a condom (sheath) which will act as a barrier. However, the condom will have to be put on carefully, with well-washed hands, to avoid infecting the outer surface of the sheath which would come in contact with the woman's body. If a new partner is not cooperative, then inserting contraceptive foam, jelly or cream into the vagina *may* destroy the venereal organisms as well as the sperm, but it does not always work.

It has also been suggested that after a casual encounter and possible exposure to a venereal infection, it may help to urinate immediately after intercourse and then wash the genital area with soap and water. Urine is usually acid and so may help to discourage the growth of some pathogenic organisms, which tend to favour an alkalinic environment and the soap and water may wash out or kill off other organisms, but these procedures, too, cannot really be relied on.

Seeking medical help

Finally, at the first signs of abnormal symptoms, do seek medical help, preferably from a VD clinic, as doctors who work there are more experienced in this field and have the facilities to make an immediate and accurate diagnosis. Many large hospitals have such clinics or can tell you where the nearest one is. You can then accept with confidence their reassurance that all is well, or if not, then the most effective treatment can be started immediately. After that it is up to you to report conscientiously for any further treatment or check-ups that are offered and thus prevent relapse, complications and subsequent disability and even disablement.

Are there vaccinations against venereal diseases?

A vaccine against genital herpes is being developed in America and should become available within the next few years. It is claimed to be effective in preventing the disease but is less effective as a complete cure for those already infected. Apparently, it does reduce the severity of attacks.

As yet there are no effective vaccines against syphilis and gonorrhoea which are the most damaging venereal diseases. Nor are there vaccines available for the other, milder conditions.

It is up to every sexually active person to be aware that all these diseases are widespread and can be easily picked up from even one casual act of intercourse with a new partner. Knowing this, both men and women who do not confine themselves to one partner should seek regular check-ups. Shyness need not be a deterrent – the doctors are more interested in your genital health than in your name or face! In some venereal clinics, on admission patients are given numbers and after that names are never used when attending subsequent sessions. But even if this is not the practice at your clinic, it should not deter you from attending, because the risk of the alternatives can be extremely serious.

Can love-making set off labour?

In a normal pregnancy it is not easy to set off a labour before it is naturally due. Even doctors have not yet found a perfect way of doing it. This is why when doctors have to induce labour for any good medical reason, they combine two drastic methods to try to ensure success: a surgical method, which involves artificially rupturing the membranes surrounding the baby; and a medical method, which involves dripping a pituitary hormone into the woman's circulation. Even then labour does not necessarily always follow immediately and the hormone drip either has to be increased in strength, or repeated a day or so later. If all this fails, as it may, the pregnancy may then have to be ended by doing a Caesarean operation.

The crucial factor as to whether labour can be set off or not is the state of the cervix. Towards the end of pregnancy – any time within three weeks of the due birth date – the condition of the cervix begins to change. Instead of being long and thick, it softens, shortens and thins out in preparation for opening up when labour starts. The cervix is then described as being 'ripe' and this only occurs when labour is naturally imminent. Before the cervix is 'ripe' a medical induction will not start the labour, as the following example shows:

> (The consultant) said that the head was in the brim and well down and in his view it was quite a large baby, so suggested an induction . . . .
>
> Anyway, that evening I had an enema and a hot bath – still hoping the baby would start on its own – slept really well and awoke full of eager anticipation. The next morning (today) I was taken to the labour ward and the drip was set up. Nothing happened . . . I feel bitterly disappointed and had a good cry afterwards but I am all right now . . . The doctor seems to think I may well go into labour myself now and he is going to see if there is any change on Friday.

The drip was again administered a few days later with the same negative result. She eventually started labour spontaneously eighteen days after the due date.

So, if all is well with the pregnancy then love-making alone cannot set off labour before the cervix is ripe. On the other hand, once the cervix is ripe, then virtually anything is likely to trigger off labour, and this includes love-making. But by then the baby is considered to be fully grown, ready to be born and capable of surviving outside the uterus. In fact, at that stage some couples even use intercourse as a form of 'natural' induction!

I was told at the clinic that I would have to be taken in for induction on 11 March as the baby would then be five days overdue, so I was naturally anxious for labour to start before then, so suggested to my husband that we could go to bed and try your 'patent method'. Accordingly, we made love and the result was instantaneous and dramatic success!

It is possible to ripen the cervix artificially by placing a prostaglandin pessary high up in the vagina near the cervix:

I was taken down to the labour ward at 8.30 am on Monday to be induced with prostaglandin . . . The prostaglandins were inserted and the heart/contraction monitor was put on me.

After two hours I walked back to the ward with a nurse. I had been told to walk around as much as possible as this would help my labour to start.

After walking around all morning, I started to get back and stomach ache. By 4 pm I was getting contractions every twenty minutes. My membranes ruptured at 4.30 pm and my contractions were now coming very regularly!

What causes a premature labour?

A labour is considered to be premature in a pregnancy of more than 28 weeks but less than 37 weeks duration (i.e. 6½-8½ months). And any baby that weighs less than 5½ lbs (2.5 kg) at birth or is less than 18 inches (46.5 cm) long is treated as a premature baby.

The course of a premature labour is very much the same as that of a labour at full term – even though the baby may be very small.

In about half the cases of premature labour, there is no obvious reason for the early ending of the pregnancy. And for many women a premature labour is an isolated occurrence and all their other babies tend to be born when they are full term.

There are, however, a small percentage of women who, in spite of abstaining from intercourse and in spite of all efforts by their doctors, still tend to produce all their babies early. Sometimes each following pregnancy ends earlier than the previous one and each succeeding baby therefore tends to be smaller than his/her brothers and sisters. There is as yet no solution to this sad problem and these mothers need very special antenatal care to help keep the pregnancy going as near to full term as possible.

Known causes of premature labour

1. Some serious illness in the mother, e.g. heart disease, kidney disease, severe toxaemia of pregnancy, diabetes, abnormalities and disease of the uterus, etc. Even a temporary acute illness with a high temperature may cause the woman to go into early labour.

2. Women who are malnourished or anaemic tend to have a higher incidence of premature births.

3. Early separation of the placenta from the wall of the uterus will result in bleeding and may lead to labour starting. This also applies to a low-lying placenta that covers the cervix.

4. If the placenta is not functioning well, is diseased (e.g. syphilitic), or is in any way abnormal, then the baby is not getting enough nourishment and may be born prematurely.

5. A damaged cervix may begin to open prematurely.

6. Over-distension of the uterus due to a multiple pregnancy (this is why twins tend to come early) or over-distension because there is an abnormal amount of amniotic fluid.

7. A malformed foetus which did not come away as a miscarriage is usually delivered prematurely.

8. The rhesus factor or other blood-grouping imcompatibilities.

9. Severe emotional stress, such as shock, which leads to physical and biochemical changes in the body may result in premature labour, e.g. shock after a car accident, or shock after hearing very bad news.

10. Women who are heavy smokers tend to have smaller babies and babies who are born prematurely. Smoking constricts the blood vessels so that less nutrients and oxygen get through to the placenta and thus to the baby. It has been suggested that the baby's blood vessels can be similarly affected.

Women who fall into any of the above categories and are therefore at risk of going into a premature labour should, early in pregnancy, be given specific guidance by the doctor about intercourse. If you are at all worried, then do ask your doctor for explanations, information, reassurance and guidance.

One line of action which can do no harm but may help to maintain the pregnancy, is to take vitamin E. With her doctor's permission, the woman at risk could take a daily dose of 200-300 international units and should continue taking vitamin E throughout her pregnancy.

It is not always easy or even possible to stop a premature labour once it has started. For a few women, however, an unorthodox treatment which was successful was acupuncture:

Having produced my first baby four weeks prematurely, I was alarmed when there were signs of labour starting ten weeks in advance of the expected date of my second. I had been to the doctor's earlier that day and they had said that the baby's head was engaged and that I should get in touch with the hospital if there were signs of labour starting. Later that day contractions started . . . another girl who had been to an acupuncturist in a similar situation . . . put me in touch with him, and the next day, with the contractions becoming more insistent, I very apprehensively went to see him. He agreed (after an external examination) that labour seemed imminent. The treatment lasted about 45 minutes and afterwards I felt much more relaxed, the contractions ceased, and the baby's head had disengaged. He said I might easily need another treatment, and to return if necessary.

I went into labour again about four weeks later: this time it progressed much more rapidly and I decided to go to the hospital rather than the acupuncturist.

I sometimes wonder whether it would have been better to go to the acupuncturist immediately signs of labour started, as my son was only 4 lb 11 oz and had to spend the first three weeks in hospital gaining weight.

Even if a premature labour is inevitable, adequate and competent care can still ensure a satisfactory outcome. Here is a graphic description of a premature birth that was handled by both the obstetrician and nursing staff in not only a competent but also a concerned and caring way.

The baby (the mother's seventh pregnancy and 4th live birth) was born in the thirty-first week of gestation and weighed 2 lb 1 oz (950g, i.e. less than one kilogram)! The fact that a baby so tiny and so premature was able to survive at all was only possible because of the superb care given both to his mother in labour and to him after birth. The birth took place under the National Health Service in March 1977 and the child is perfectly normal and flourishing:

I was admitted at 11 pm on the 17 March, extremely tired and glad to feel that we were in the best possible place. At five the next morning I awoke, sticky and bleeding. The obstetrician was notified at sixish and I was moved to the labour ward. Throughout the period between awakening and the obstetrician arriving (about 7.30 am) I was treated with care, consideration for my worries and a lot of foresight was shown (i.e. blood was matched, a drip set up to keep a vein open, etc.).

As soon as I was installed in the labour ward someone came to ask if she could telephone my husband, someone else installed a monitor and bothered to ask if I would like it explained, the obstetrician's houseman reassured me that no drugs would be given (as I had previously, the evening

before, agreed with the obstetrician that it would be better
for the baby not to use pethidine routinely). I was never left
alone and when one midwife 'passed' me on to another she
took the trouble to say that I did not like to have my
contractions referred to as pains!

The obstetrician arrived when I was contracting about
every three minutes. Good contractions, building up quite
quickly. I remember feeling irritated when a midwife stood
between me and my fixed point (her focus of concentration)!
From the time that he (the obstetrician) arrived I felt we
could relax totally and get on with as little worry as possible.
He took over and I knew I could concentrate. Somebody
tried to take my blood pressure in mid-contraction and he
stopped that happening, all so quietly done. The obstetrician
moved me into the delivery room earlier than is usual in
other hospitals because he feels that moving women during
transition (the difficult period between the first and second
stages of labour) is disturbing for them.

Then, after fifteen minutes in the delivery room,
transition started. With me it begins with a sense of
euphoria. The room was so peaceful. Me, the obstetrician,
the paediatric registrar and a midwife. We talked and joked
and looked at the trees outside and remembered the other
children and, although we were all aware of the risk to a
child being born so early, the atmosphere was a relaxed one.
They and I knew that I could be obedient and that there was
no need of drugs. The contractions came and I welcomed
each one. In between we talked or rested. I wanted drinks
which I could not have because of the risk of theatre if the
baby needed quick extraction. Nothing was distressful. The
urge to push could be controlled in spite of a drip board on
my arm which prevented me panting into cupped hands (a
technique for controlling the urge to bear down). I wanted
extra pillows and the obstetrician fetched them for me by
instinct. I got slightly tearful and shivery and he wiped my
eyes and held my leg during those horrid half contractions of
transition. Second stage was so long coming because of an

anterior lip of cervix that insisted on holding fast.

Eventually I could push. At this point the baby showed his first signs of 'I Want Out'. His heartbeat fell from 150 or so to 80 or so. Not good. The obstetrician got the first half of his forceps in and, to my great shame, I could not let him get the other half in. When one is working hard to get something out it demands a lot to let something quite big in! So we managed without. He was born in two contractions, almost three. I was told not to push and (being Sylvia Close trained) I stopped, and then to push hard. The contraction was fading and I remember saying that I couldn't and hearing from the obstetrician that I *could* and, of course, I did and the baby was born and I touched him and he was so tiny and the obstetrician stood up by my head and supported my shoulders so that I could see the paediatrician working on him. Little tiny perfect love and he breathed unaided. He sounded like a kitten. He was taken over for oxygen in case it was needed, which it wasn't, and the obstetrician went on holding me, telling me that his colour had changed so quickly (a good sign) and then the most reassuring sound of all: the paediatric registrar laughed: 'The little so-and-so is trying to suck my finger'.

The baby was given to me then and the obstetrician pulled up my gown to let him nuzzle at my nipple – my breast was much bigger than his head and still he attempted to take it on.

The baby then went to the special care unit and the obstetrician and I were left with a retained placenta. It was removed under a general (anaesthetic), weighed 9 oz (normal weight is about 1½ lbs) and very granulated, totally useless. Thank God the baby decided that it was better out than in.

I came round from the general (anaesthetic) feeling morbid . . . There was no reassurance – the staff did their best to help – until my husband got to me. We were given tea during which a nurse from the SCU (special care unit) came up to see us and tell us that the baby was producing no problems and that as soon as we were ready she would organize a chair to take me/us down and we could see the consultant paediatrician who would be glad to see and talk to us.

After that life became possible again and we could talk quite realistically and rationally both with the staff and with each other. The relief of knowing that people can be honest is so profound.

In spite of the fact that my husband was not present at the birth (the only one he has missed) this was the most beautiful delivery we've had. It was so calm.

I cannot remember one thing that happened during the time that I was in the hospital, or since, that was unreasonable, inconsiderate, or irrational. I feel we had the best of both scientific and instinctive care.

The prem. unit has encouraged me to keep on expressing (breast milk). Because I gave birth in the thirty-first week, it was very difficult to bring the milk in. I have managed so far because I had the confidence of having done it before, and because I knew that the staff there also regarded it as so important for the baby.

He is now almost 3 lbs and doing very well. Most important for both his well-being and mine and ours is that there is a bond between us established by the uninterrupted link that the hospital staff could so easily have destroyed instead of fostering.

Placental dysfunction

A similar problem to prematurity is placental dysfunction, also known as placental insufficiency. In this condition the placenta fails to function normally and does not convey adequate nourishment to the developing baby. This results in a baby who, although born at full term, is undernourished and weighs less than 5½ lbs. Such a baby also needs special care after birth.

One woman who had this problem in both her pregnancies is convinced that vitamin E helped her second pregnancy and baby. Here she relates her experience:

My first baby was seven days overdue and weighed only 5 lb 7 oz. His condition at birth was only fair, he was extremely sleepy and would not feed properly. He spent the first four days in the Special Care Unit, where I went to feed him three-hourly. The midwife said that the placenta was very poor and that it was doubtful that it would have functioned for much longer than another 48 hours. As a result of this I was very concerned about placental function in my second pregnancy.

The second scan indicated the baby's size to be indicative of a pregnancy three weeks behind my dates and first scan. You, of course, reassured me, reminded me of the margin of error in dates, and suggested that vitamin E – 100 mgs twice daily – might help as there is some evidence to indicate that it can improve and maintain the placenta.

After a few days I felt much fitter myself and felt I was at last doing something positive towards improving the condition of the placenta.

At the next visit to the clinic the consultant decided to admit me to stay in hospital until delivery, for foetal monitoring and rest. He said that if the baby was going to arrive late, any deterioration of the placenta would immediately show up on the (monitoring machine), and I would then be induced.

When I first went into hospital, the midwives commented about the extremely tiny baby they could feel and I felt quite despondent. However, after the first week in hospital they were all saying how the baby had suddenly grown and that it was no longer such a tiny baby! This was approximately three weeks after commencing vitamin E.

The baby also became very active whereas before he was not terribly active, and only seemed to move when I was at rest.

The baby, another little boy, was eventually born on the 16th July, after a normal delivery with no drugs, and weighed 5 lbs 15¾ oz. His condition throughout labour and at birth was good, and the placenta was good except for a small area, which was not surprising as it had functioned for another sixteen days!

He was extremely alert from the time he was born. In fact, one of the girls in my unit commented on how active he was, especially as he was smaller than the rest of the babies. I had no problems with breast-feeding, and we were both discharged home on the fourth day.

Part 2 After Childbirth

How soon after the baby's birth can intercourse be resumed?

The period after delivery is known as the puerperium. It is the time of recovery and is generally considered to last six to eight weeks, because it takes that length of time for the uterus to shrink back to almost its pre-pregnancy size, shape and position in the pelvis. The post-natal check-up is timed to be done at the end of this period and, until quite recently, couples were advised to abstain from intercourse during the puerperium.

It takes less time, however, for the cervix to close and for the vagina to return to normal – about two to three weeks – and it is now generally accepted that a couple can resume intercourse as soon as the woman feels ready to do so.

Occasionally the genital tract continues to be tender for several weeks after delivery, and this may even persist after the postnatal examination. This tenderness is quite apart from any discomfort which may be caused by stitches in the perineum (the area between the vagina and the anus) which should heal within five to ten days. Because of the tenderness, vaginal lubrication may be temporarily inhibited. But neither of these minor problems need deter a couple from resuming intercourse if care is taken to find a comfortable position, a lubricating jelly is used, and the man is gentle and considerate.

As in all things, reactions after childbirth vary considerably. I have known one woman whose sexual urge was so strong that she discharged herself and her baby from hospital on the fifth day after giving birth, solely because of her need to have intercourse. Some, on the other hand, may remain sexually apathetic for several months. Most women fit in between these two extremes and resume love-making in the second or third week after delivery:

It was two weeks after our baby was born that we first made love again, and pregnancy and childbirth certainly haven't robbed it of any of its former appeal. Really, I would have been ready – physically and emotionally – sooner than that, I wouldn't have known I'd had stitches, but I suppose the combination of being busy or tired, and not having got organized enough to do the appropriate shopping (I'd prefer a little time to get to know the baby!!) delayed things until I'd been home a week.

Sometimes women have unrealistic fears about being hurt and they need gentle persuasion and help to regain confidence to resume sexual activity:

After the birth I wasn't all that interested. If it wasn't for my husband I probably still wouldn't be interested. We made love three weeks after the birth when my stitches had healed. I enjoyed it so much that we are quite back to normal now (I had been frightened of being hurt after the birth and when I realized it didn't hurt I was back to being a sex maniac again but to a milder degree than previously).

It should, of course, be mentioned that although the menstrual cycle may not become established for some months after childbirth, nevertheless there is a definite risk of conceiving a new pregnancy in the meantime, even during the puerperium. I have personal knowledge of one young woman in her twenties who had full-term babies in March and December of one year and in

September of the following year. None of these babies was planned or wanted. This particular woman happened to be a social problem and was generally irresponsible, but this example does show that conception during the puerperium is possible and that some form of contraception should therefore always be used, unless, of course, another pregnancy is desired immediately.

Is intercourse advisable while the lochia discharge is still present?

The vaginal discharge after childbirth is called the lochia and it begins immediately after the placenta is expelled. It is in fact fresh bleeding from the placental site inside the uterus and is therefore bright red in colour. As the days pass and the uterus continues to contract and compress the blood vessels that had been feeding the placenta there is less bleeding from the placental site and, by the second week after the birth, the lochia becomes reddish-brown in colour and less in amount. The lochia continues to get darker in colour and more scanty until it stops completely. This may happen any time from three weeks onwards, or it may gradually peter out throughout the puerperium and stop completely at about the time of the postnatal examination. By then it will be just a slight black mark on the sanitary pad.

If at any time within the puerperium (i. e. within 8 weeks of the baby's birth) the lochia becomes bright red again, do report this to your doctor. There is always the possibility that the uterus has relaxed a little and that the bright red discharge is fresh bleeding from the placental site. This should not be ignored as it may lead to a serious haemorrhage. The doctor will either reassure you that all is well or prescribe medication to help the uterus contract, which in turn will control the bleeding.

Love-making may in fact help the uterus to contract strongly, because oxytocin (one of the pituitary hormones) is released when the woman has an orgasm, and makes the uterus contract.

Oxytocin is also released when the baby sucks at the breast and this is why the internal organs of the woman who breast-feeds return to normal more quickly than those of the woman who bottle-feeds her baby.

Making love while the lochia is still present is very much a personal choice: some couples find it aesthetically unacceptable while others are not at all affected by it. Most couples rely on the sheath for contraceptive protection during the puerperium and this also acts as a protection against the lochia which some men could find physically irritating.

What causes sexual apathy after childbirth?

Quite a considerable number of women experience sexual apathy in the weeks and early months after giving birth. It may even happen to those who previously had a strong sex drive. There is no one specific cause but many factors can contribute and predispose to this temporary state.

Childbirth can at times be a stressful and even a traumatic experience, especially if the woman has not been adequately prepared for the event beforehand. Many women have unrealistic expectations of childbirth and for them – even if the labour is normal – the reality of the event can be a rude awakening. These women are more liable to feelings of disappointment and even guilt about not having been able to cope adequately with labour. The disillusionment that follows, and the fear of having to repeat the traumatic childbirth experience, may make the woman disinclined to make love. For her, sexual apathy is then simply a protective mechanism (though not a conscious one) against another pregnancy and childbirth.

Women who have had difficult or complicated labours and who needed obstetric help (such as forceps or a caesarean operation) to deliver the baby, may take longer to recover completely – physically, emotionally and sexually.

Another reason for sexual apathy is fear of being hurt. Mostly the fear relates to the genital area but occasionally anxiety is centred on the breasts:

> I have found it extremely difficult to respond to my husband sexually – as much for physical reasons as any more complicated ones. Firstly, while breast-feeding, my breasts feel uncomfortable whenever they are touched or pressed against and it's quite difficult to avoid any contact during love-making and I feel tense in case my husband accidentally touches my breasts or else simply forgets in the heat of the moment. Secondly, I feel almost frightened since having the baby that things are not back to normal and even as I write these notes (eight weeks after delivery) full sexual intercourse has not taken place mainly due to my fear of being hurt.
>
> I felt exactly the same after my first son was born, and all the time I was breast-feeding – some fifteen months – intercourse was something to be avoided. Once I stopped feeding him, however, all 'normal' feelings returned and our love life was just as good as it had been previously.

Episiotomies

The current trend to inflict episiotomies on almost all women – even those who have perfectly normal labours and deliveries – may well be another predisposing cause. An episiotomy is a small cut (about 1 inch or 25 mm long) in the lower part of the vagina. Its purpose is to enlarge the opening and facilitate delivery, and this is fine when it is necessary. However, problems arise if the episiotomy is afterwards incompetently repaired (stitched). This, of course, should never happen but all too frequently it does, and women complain bitterly and resentfully about pain and discomfort when walking, sitting, and later on when making love. What makes matters worse is that instead of healing within seven to ten days, as do well-repaired episiotomies, those that have been badly repaired continue to give trouble for weeks and sometimes months later even after the cut has healed:

> . . . the senior registrar popped in to congratulate me on the birth, I requested he do the episiotomy as a favour . . . as he sutured he made a joke about suturing the patients slightly tight so their husbands would have a better sex life.
>
> It was fourteen weeks after the birth before my husband and I had sexual intercourse. It was very painful.
>
> It was eighteen weeks before the next time. It took months before it was comfortable.
>
> My baby is now seven months old and I still find intercourse slightly painful on entry.
>
> 'That's no joke' is exactly what I would say to that registrar next time we meet.

Sometimes the stitching has been so botched that the woman needs an operation under a general anaesthetic to correct the damage:

> My first baby was born after a long and difficult labour aided by forceps. I had what the midwife described as 'rather a lot' of stitches as a result of the episiotomy.
>
> After the birth I had great difficulty in sitting down, but as everyone else in the ward seemed to be suffering similarly I didn't think too much of it.
>
> I came home delighted with my son and clutching antibiotics because of a minor infection in the stitch line. I still couldn't sit properly and even the weight of my son on my lap caused distress. When the midwife called she removed several stitches to make life easier. After a few weeks I could sit down without wincing. At my postnatal examination I told the doctor that all didn't feel well 'down below' and that an attempt at love-making had to be abandoned because of pain. He realized the truth of this

when he tried to examine me internally and gave up as I nearly went up the wall. 'All will be well soon' I was told.

All was not well. When baby was four months old love-making was still extremely painful and generally avoided. I went to my GP and she gave me steroid cream which I hopefully and conscientiously applied – no difference at all. I was in despair now as I thought that nothing else could be done for me so I didn't go back to the GP for quite a while.

When I went to see her again she suggested that I see a gynaecologist. Great idea, I thought. However, the earliest I could get a non-urgent appointment was three to four months ahead. I was horrified and so was my long-suffering husband.

The only solution was to arrange a private consultation. I saw the gynaecologist within a week! He said that some nerve endings might have been trapped and that the scar tissue should be removed. Three weeks later I was in hospital feeling very nervous indeed. I needn't have worried as the operation was successful, but I must say that for a long time I felt very resentful about the casual attitude when I had tried to get medical help. It was, in fact, seven months after the birth of my son before our sex life was back to normal.

I'm expecting my second baby any time now so if I need an episiotomy, I hope I get a good 'needle woman'.

Fatigue

An inexperienced new mother who, in addition to her normal household chores, has to cope with a baby who does not sleep, cries a lot, or has feeding problems, will soon become tired and worn out – and of course, disinclined for sex:

After the baby was born I was very tired and felt haggard and unattractive – a slave to the baby for nearly 24 hours a day. I can't remember ever feeling like doing anything other than sleeping when I was able to get to bed!

Depression

Depression is another reason for sexual apathy. It may be the weepy low state of the postnatal blues which happens within a few days of the baby's birth. It may be a more serious full-blown depression which is associated with insomnia, anorexia (loss of appetite), hallucinations (imagining things) and a general tendency to lose touch with reality. It may also be that unrecognized grey state when all enthusiasms and zest for living have disappeared. The new mother feels worn-out, emotionally spent, disinterested and is in a general state of misery. Everything becomes an effort – getting dressed, going out, folding the nappies, etc. She functions at a very low level. This, too, is a form of depression. Adjusting to motherhood sometimes involves stresses and strains. It is also a time of great and sudden hormonal changes which can affect different women in different ways (or not at all); however, it is the *depression* which is responsible for the sexual apathy rather than the hormonal changes.

It has been suggested that, with the expulsion of the placenta, the main source of oestrogen production has been lost until the ovaries start producing it again, and that this causes the loss of sex drive. But this is an unlikely explanation for several reasons: the reduced oestrogen level is common to all women after having given birth; ovarian function can be suppressed for many months while the woman is breast-feeding her baby; the adrenal glands also produce some oestrogen; once the sex drive has been established at puberty, its continuation is dependent on emotional factors rather than the fluctuation of oestrogen production. An obvious example of this is the continuing sexual activity of postmenopausal women.

Even though the lack of interest in sex is temporary, it is nevertheless very upsetting – women worry about it and wonder if they will ever be sexually normal again. In fact, anxiety and feelings of guilt only aggravate the matter and actually delay the return to normal. The new mother needs help – practical help with regard to the baby and its problems, as well as emotional support and reassurance regarding her anxieties. With this sort of help, she will be able to overcome the predisposing factors and regain her normal healthy interest in sex. In cases of persistent depression, do seek medical help.

Is there a risk of infection from sexual intercourse too soon after the birth?

In the days before antibiotics it was a good precautionary measure to abstain from sexual intercourse during the puerperium. Then an infection in the genital area during labour or immediately after childbirth (puerperal sepsis) was very serious as there was always the risk of the infection spreading into the uterus and, through the unhealed placental site, into the general circulation to cause generalized blood poisoning (puerperal septicaemia). Without antibiotics to counteract such a massive infection, it was a matter of good nursing, as well as chance, as to whether the woman survived or not.

Fortunately, today circumstances are different. We have better standards of hygiene which minimize the risk of any genital infection and we have antibiotics tailored to deal with any specific infection which may occur. Also, women are better nourished and therefore healthier, with a higher resistance to infections.

By the time the mother returns home from the hospital the healing process is well on the way. Any stitches should have healed within ten days. The cervix will be closed (it closes rapidly after the placenta has been expelled, usually within the first two weeks). The uterus (which was on a level with the navel after the birth) will, after about ten days, have shrunk to the level of the pubic bone, though it will still take another four to six weeks to return to its pre-pregnancy size. If the woman is breast-feeding the baby, the accompanying constant release of the pituitary hormone oxytocin, will further help the uterus to shrink.

To sum up: provided the woman does not develop an infection during her stay in hospital, and provided normal general standards of hygiene are observed, then infection from intercourse with a known and healthy partner is unlikely.

Will the vagina, after stretching in labour, return to its normal size?

The vagina is a muscular passage about 3 inches or 75 mm long and is capable of great distension. Its inner lining (which is not muscle but more like a mucous membrane) is folded into ridges (rugae) to allow for stretching. The vagina is supported and kept in position mainly by two large sheets of strong muscle (lavator ani) on either side of the bony pelvis, which join together in the middle to form a muscular sling. The sling is perforated by the openings of the urethra, vagina and anus. Other muscles from the pubic bone to the coccyx and around these openings, as well as strong ligaments, help to strengthen the whole structure. This is the pelvic floor which supports and keeps in place all the pelvic organs – the bladder, the vagina and the bowel.

In labour, as the baby is pushed down and along the birth canal, the presenting part (usually the head) stretches the vagina, and the rugae open up and are flattened against the muscular vaginal walls. The vaginal opening is also distended by the presenting part, allowing the baby's head to come through. The delivery is carefully controlled by the midwife or doctor so that the distension is kept to a minimum. Sometimes the vaginal opening cannot stretch sufficiently and the tissues either tear a little or the midwife (or doctor) will do an episiotomy (a small cut) to prevent tearing and to enlarge the opening. After the birth the tear or cut will be stitched. Once a woman has had a vaginal delivery, her pelvic floor has been subjected to a greater or lesser degree of strain.

The vaginal muscles – like the muscles of the uterus, bowel, heart and other internal organs – are 'involuntary', which means they cannot consciously be tightened or relaxed at will; but the muscles of the pelvic floor consist of 'voluntary' muscles, which can be controlled at will.

Just as the uterus, which was stretched during pregnancy to accommodate the growing baby, returns to almost its pre-pregnancy size within two months of the baby's birth, so too do the vaginal muscles and the rugae return to virtually their pre-pregnancy state. Although a woman cannot actively contract the vaginal muscles, she can improve its position and state quite considerably by toning up the pelvic floor muscles. The stronger the pelvic floor muscles, the less likelihood is there that the vagina will remain distended.

Pelvic floor exercises

At their antenatal preparation classes all women should be taught how to become aware of and how to relax the pelvic floor muscles in preparation for the birth and to facilitate the delivery of the baby. The same muscles have to be toned up and strengthened again after the baby is born.

Doing a few easy exercises every day is a simple and sensible way to regain and maintain good tone in the pelvic floor muscles – not only immediately after the birth but every day throughout life. It should become a lifelong habit. It is a good preventative measure because as we get older the muscles of the body tend to lose tone and get flabby. This also applies to the pelvic floor muscles which tend to sag and this is why middle-aged and older women sometimes need gynaecological repair operations.

Since these exercises take only a few minutes to do, this is not quite as onerous a task as it may at first appear. In fact, most of them can be done whenever you have a spare moment, and in any position – standing, sitting or lying down. They should be done gently and slowly. You will need to concentrate to become aware of the muscles you are strengthening when you do the following:

1. Gently and slowly tighten the muscles controlling the opening to the bowel (as if closing the anal opening to stop the bowel emptying). Hold tight for a few seconds and then gently let go. Make sure that you do not hold your breath and do not tighten your buttock muscles or your tummy muscles at the same time.

2. Gently and slowly tighten the muscles controlling the opening to the bladder until you cannot tighten them any more and then gently let go. The best way to learn which muscles are involved is to practise when urinating. Try to control, and later to stop, the stream of urine every time you empty your bladder. Do it several times at each voiding. At first you may feel that nothing is happening but as you persevere, you will be able to slow down the stream of urine and in time you may be able to stop it completely (but even just slowing down the stream is helpful).

3. Gently and slowly contract (and release) the muscles around the vaginal opening, as if you were trying to bring the labias even closer together (i.e. from side to side). It does not matter if at first other pelvic floor muscles are also working at the same time – just concentrate on the vagina. It is a small movement but with practice you will feel it getting stronger.

4. Contract the muscles around the urethra, vagina and anus, and keeping the muscles tight, gently and slowly draw the whole pelvic floor upwards as if into your abdomen. Hold at the highest level for a few seconds and then gently let the muscles return to their normal position.

5. Estimate where the end of your spine is and then try to shorten the space between it and the pubic bone (i.e. the area from front to back) by gently and slowly drawing the tissues together. When you reach the maximum point of tightness, hold for a few seconds and then gently let go.

6. Insert a clean finger into the vagina and contract the muscles around it so that it is gripped tightly by the vagina.

With the exception of the last exercise, the others can be done so unobtrusively that no one else need be aware of what you are doing. They can even be a profitable diversion at a boring social function!

How soon after the birth does menstruation return?

There is no definite pattern for the re-establishment of the menstrual cycle after childbirth and it varies a great deal from one woman to another. To a large extent it depends on whether a woman is breast-feeding her baby or not, because the high level of prolactin (a pituitary hormone present in the circulation when the woman is breast-feeding) suppresses the other pituitary hormones that act on the ovaries, thus preventing ovulation and menstruation. In theory, therefore, breast-feeding should act as a natural contraceptive, and for some women it does. But it is the actual *level* of prolactin which is the determining factor and this can never be known to the woman herself, and is likely to fluctuate anyway. So if a couple do not want another baby in nine months time then it would be wise to use some method of contraception and not rely on chance and the hope that the level of prolactin is adequate for inhibiting ovulation.

If a woman is not breast-feeding her baby, then the first ovulation can occur about a month after giving birth, and menstruation will follow two weeks later, i.e. when the baby is six to seven weeks old. Most women (whether they breast-feed or not) begin to menstruate when the baby is between three and six months old.

Some women who breast-feed do not menstruate for the whole duration of the breast-feeding period, which is usually nine months. Then there are those women who, without having established their menstrual cycle, become pregnant again and so menstruation is again suppressed for another year, or possibly longer if they also breast-feed the next baby. Pregnancy is possible in the latter case either because the pituitary hormones were beginning to work normally or because of spontaneous ovulation (when having an orgasm) which can happen to women under 35 years of age.

No matter when the woman starts to menstruate again, it sometimes takes a few months for the normal rhythm of her cycle to become established. This means that the first few periods may not only be irregular in time, but the flow may also be heavier than normal. If a woman is anxious about either of these aspects, then she should seek reassurance from her doctor, but usually the process sorts itself out and stabilizes after a few cycles.

Why does menstruation vary so much?

Menstruation is only one part of a very delicately balanced and complex system which involves the brain (hypothalamus), the pituitary gland, the ovaries and the uterus (both the inner lining and the cervix). It also affects the breasts, the vagina and fallopian tubes and involves moods, emotions, appetites, ability to concentrate and most aspects of a woman's being.

To understand the complexity of the subject, we need to start at the beginning. When a girl baby is born, each one of her two tiny ovaries already contains thousands of potential eggs (ova). Each egg (ovum) encased in a little container of cells is called a follicle.

At puberty the reproductive system is triggered into activity by the hypothalamus and begins to work cyclically. Each month the hypothalamus signals the pituitary gland to release two hormones – the follicle-stimulating hormone (FSH) and the luteinizing hormone (LH). The follicle-stimulating hormone acts on a crop of follicles in the ovary. These follicles begin to ripen. Special cells secrete the hormone oestrogen, fluid collects inside the follicle and the egg matures. As the whole structure enlarges, it also forces its way to the surface of the ovary.

Although several follicles (now called graafian follicles) are affected by the FSH, only one (occasionally two) actually ripens to full maturity. The others lose the race, collapse and regress.

When the winning graafian follicle reaches full maturity it looks like a little blister bulging out of the ovary, and inside the little blister is the ripe ovum. By now the level of oestrogen is very high and this triggers the pituitary gland to release a sudden spurt of the luteinizing hormone. It is the LH that causes the graafian follicle to burst and release the ripe ovum – this is the moment of ovulation. The released ovum is drawn or sucked into the fallopian tube and is propelled along the tube to the uterus.

Before ovulation occurs, the increased amount of oestrogen from the ripening graafian follicles affects the inner lining of the uterus (endometrium); new cells develop and grow, making the whole lining much, much thicker. After ovulation the empty ruptured graafian follicle under the influence of the LH undergoes changes (including its name – it is now called the corpus luteum) and begins to secrete the hormone progesterone as well as some oestrogen. Progesterone not only maintains the new thick lining in the uterus but also causes it to swell and become more spongy, with the creation of tiny cavities containing glycogen-rich fluid. All these changes in the endometrium are for the sole purpose of receiving and sustaining a fertilized egg. The corpus luteum continues to secrete progesterone and oestrogen and so maintains the pregnancy until the placenta is fully developed three months later, when it can take over this function as well as that of nourishing the developing baby. Once implantation has occurred it is in fact the fertilized egg that secretes a substance (human chorionic gonadotrophin – HCG) which keeps the corpus luteum functioning. It is therefore the presence of HCG in the urine which gives a positive sign of pregnancy.

If, however, the egg is not fertilized, then the corpus luteum begins to shrivel up and the level of progesterone and oestrogen falls. Without the support of these ovarian hormones, the new spongy lining inside the uterus becomes detached and is expelled together with the ovum and some blood as the menstrual flow. Menstruation has actually been described as 'the weeping of a disappointed uterus'!

The fall in the level of the ovarian hormones triggers off the release of FSH and LH from the anterior lobe of the pituitary gland again and this acts on another crop of ovarian follicles and the whole cycle is thus repeated month after month. It is disrupted naturally by pregnancy, lactation and the onset of the menopause. It can also be disrupted by illness, metabolic disturbances, emotional crises, malnutrition, travel, the stress of changing jobs, and other stresses, as well as the contraceptive pill.

The normal menstrual cycle is estimated as being 28 days, i.e. fourteen days from the first day of the last period to the day of ovulation and fourteen days from the day of ovulation until the day before the onset of the next period. The post-ovulatory period does not vary and is constant at fourteen days. But the pre-ovulatory period can vary a great deal, ranging from seven to 28 days (or more). This is due entirely to individual differences in the way the body works. So with seven to 28 pre-ovulation days, plus the constant fourteen post-ovulation days, the result is a cycle that can vary from 21-42 days. The duration of menstrual bleeding also varies, averaging between three to seven days.

It is the hypothalamus, responding to signals from the autonomic nervous system, which initiates and controls the whole process. This, too, varies between individuals, with some women being more easily affected than others, and helps to account for individual variations and disruptions in menstrual patterns.

What are the various methods of contraception?

There is as yet no perfect method of contraception. All methods currently practised have both advantages and disadvantages and some are now known to be actually injurious to health.

The effectiveness of most of the methods depends entirely on the woman – so the burden of preventing an unwanted pregnancy falls on her.

In choosing a method of contraception, the first priority should be to ensure that the woman does not in any way jeopardize her health. Unfortunately, women all too often opt for a particular method of contraception simply because it is 'easy', or react with distaste to another method merely because it is 'messy'. These are clearly not intelligent criteria in a subject of such importance to not only one's immediate but also one's long-term healthy fertile life.

The contraceptive pill

Methods of contraception are based on a variety of principles. The contraceptive pill, which has in the last two decades become very popular, is based on the principle of preventing ovulation. If there is no ripe ovum, then there cannot be a baby. To ensure that ovulation does not occur, it becomes necessary to completely disrupt a woman's delicately-balanced hormonal functioning, which would normally and naturally lead to ovulation. This is achieved by the woman swallowing daily a high dose of synthetic hormones contained in the pill. In other words, the pill suppresses the cyclic production of natural ovarian hormones and substitutes a high level of artificial ones which suppress ovulation. And in addition, of course, the natural cyclical fluctuation of hormones is disrupted.

The composition of the pill varies slightly from one brand to another but there are four main types.

1. *The combined pill*
This is the most common. Each pill contains both oestrogen and progestogen (synthetic progesterone) and is taken daily for about 21 days from the first day of the cycle. It affects fertility in several ways: the high level of synthetic hormones suppresses the pituitary hormones and stops ovulation; it interferes with the

normal cyclic maturation of the uterine lining so that implantation cannot occur; it affects the cervical mucus making it thick, viscid and impenetrable to sperm.

Bleeding occurs regularly every 28 days no matter what the previous cycle was. Because of the altered physiology and suppression of normal function, the bleeding is not true menstruation; it is shorter in duration and less in amount. Even if bleeding stops completely, it does not necessarily imply that the woman is pregnant.

2. The sequential pill

This pill is also taken for 21 days. It contains oestrogen for the first fifteen to sixteen days and then oestrogen and progestogen for the other six to five days, thus mimicking the natural production of hormones, but at a higher level. It is, however, associated with endometrial cancer in some women and has therefore been withdrawn from sale in many countries, including America and Britain.

3. The triphasic pill

This is a new pill, and although it contains a higher dose of oestrogen, the total amount of hormones is lower than in either of the above two types. The 21 pills that have to be taken in every cycle are divided into three unequal lots of six, five, and ten pills. Each lot is a different colour and contains a different dose of oestrogen and progestogen. The purpose is to reproduce, as far as possible, the natural rise and fall of hormone levels and thereby to reduce side-effects. It is thus very important to take the pills in the order prescribed by the manufacturer or they may not be effective.

4. The mini-pill

This pill contains progestogen only and is taken daily without a break. Unlike the other pills, the mini-pill does not usually suppress ovulation,[1] instead its main contraceptive effect is to

---

[1] Only a high level of progestogen will suppress ovulation.

thicken the cervical mucus so that sperm cannot get through. It may also affect the uterine lining and prevent implantation if by chance an egg is fertilized. But sometimes it fails:

> I conceived whilst taking the contraceptive mini-pill. I had been taking this pill for one month and three weeks before intercourse took place so was well covered as the 'unsafe' period until it takes effect is fourteen days.
> I was taking no other form of drugs or medication at that time and took the pill regularly at 7 pm each day without a break.

Side-effects of the pill

Many pill-users naïvely believe that the pill only affects the ovaries. But the pill contains powerful chemicals that are absorbed into the circulation, carried throughout the body and are thus also liable to affect every system and organ in the body. This is why so many different side-effects have been reported. Different women react differently to the same drug and the side-effects of the pill also vary from woman to woman. They may be minor or serious, and some side-effects take a long time to come to light. It is important that women who choose to take the contraceptive pill should have regular health checks at least once a year, but preferably every six months.

Many women do tolerate the pill well. Nevertheless, as the pill affects body chemistry, all pill-users should be aware of possible side-effects which include:

—spotting or break-through bleeding (i.e. bleeding between periods)
—bloating and swelling of fingers and ankles
—nausea
—congestion and tenderness of the breasts
—fatigue and lethargy
—mood changes – nervousness, irritability, depression
—weight gain, which may be due either to fluid retention or increase in fat and muscle

—headache, migraine or visual disturbances
—altered sex drive
—skin changes – sensitivity to light, dark markings on face, small
    nodules under the skin
—inflammation and bleeding of the gums
—mouth ulcers
—varicose veins may enlarge
—metabolic changes which can result in easy bruising, allergic
    reactions, vitamin and mineral deficiencies (e.g. of vitamin
    B_6, folic acid, vitamin C, zinc etc.)
—lowered resistance to infections leading to more urinary tract
    infections, vaginal infection more likely to spread to pelvis,
    vaginitis and fungal infections:

After being on the pill for a short time I discovered, after
visiting my doctor, that I had 'thrush', something I knew
nothing about, until I was reassured it was nothing serious –
just one of the side-effects of taking the pill. I was prescribed
a course of pessaries, which did clear it up, thank goodness,
as it was most uncomfortable and sometimes quite painful.
Since then, however, I have had 'thrush' repeatedly every
year, while taking the pill.

The second time I suffered with it, the doctor again
prescribed pessaries, and also tablets, which my husband also
had to take. This again cleared the problem within a short
time. But I was told that as long as I carried on taking the pill,
I would probably always suffer with thrush.

—diabetes
—epilepsy may be triggered off or existing epilepsy made worse
—changes in the cervix, possibly resulting in cervical pathology
—gall bladder disorders
—altered liver function and pathology – jaundice, tumours
—blood vessel changes which can lead to serious complications
    like high blood-pressure, kidney damage, strokes
—benign uterine fibroids tend to enlarge
—early cancer of the breast or cervix can be aggravated

—alteration of the blood-clotting mechanism, which can result in thrombosis, pulmonary embolism, strokes, or heart attacks. (After an operation there is more risk of deep vein thrombosis and for this reason the pill should be stopped at least one month, preferably two, before any surgical operation.)

—post-pill infertility. This is fairly common but is usually a temporary state. If it persists, the woman may need treatment

—a combination of side-effects:

I took the first pill I was prescribed for about a year without any side-effects. For no apparent reason I became very depressed. My GP changed the pill I was using to another brand. I took this one for about four-and-a-half years. During the four-and-a-half years I put on about a stone in weight and suffered a slightly higher blood-pressure than normal. During the last six months I was on the pill I began to suffer pins and needles in my legs. I also suffered numbness in my face. My local family planning clinic suggested that I stopped using the pill. I was fitted with the contraceptive diaphragm. I used this until we decided to try for a family.

—altered function of the thyroid gland. This is a less common side-effect, but nevertheless a serious one in susceptible subjects, as described in the following account:

I took the pill for three years. After that time my husband and I decided to try for our first baby. I conceived within twelve weeks of my last prescription and from the first, unknown to me at the time, was feeling the symptoms of thyrotoxicosis (palpitations, shaking hands, protruding eyes, etc.). Although complaining of these symptoms to my GP the problem was not diagnosed until I was five months pregnant by which time I was severely affected by the toxicity of my thyroid gland.

The gland was X-rayed, a very worrying experience even

though I wore a lead apron, and I had to take six 5mg tablets of a thyroid depressant per day, the maximum dose for a pregnant woman. But even this dose did not control the problem totally, but because of my condition no other treatment was offered. It was during this time that I learnt of the pill being connected with causing over-activity of the thyroid gland. During this period it was decided that careful monitoring should take place of the baby and I was in and out of hospital for this to be done. As the pregnancy reached the latter stages it was recommended the drugs should be reduced so that if possible I would not be taking any when the baby was delivered thus reducing the chances of the baby being born with the opposite condition to that which I had. I also wanted to stop taking the drugs so that I could breast-feed the baby (the drugs cause immunity problems in the breast-fed infant).

The baby was born with no thyroid problems but did have the neural tube defect (mild spina bifida) which I have already mentioned to you. After her delivery I was strongly advised not to use the pill because of being thyrotoxic. I breast-fed her for four months but then had to take the drugs again as I was becoming affected once more. She is now approaching her second birthday and I am still taking the drugs and because of this I must not conceive as the thyroid-depressant drugs affect cell division in the first twelve weeks of life.

It may be possible by manipulating the dosage of hormones (i.e., changing the brand of pill) to correct some of the milder side-effects. But women should not attempt to treat symptoms on their own for two reasons: the drugs they take may interact with and reduce the efficacy of the pill; it is better to allow the body to right itself and return to normal by changing to another method of contraception rather than take drugs to counteract other drugs.

Contra-indications for the pill
Because of the many possible and serious effects, the contraceptive pill is unsuitable for:

1. Young girls who are still growing and whose hormonal functioning is not yet completely mature, as the pill may suppress normal bone growth and hormonal development.

2. Women who have irregular or scanty periods, as they may not regain their ovulation or menstruation after stopping the pill.

3. Women aged 35 (some say 30) and older, especially if they are heavy smokers as they are more liable to sudden heart attacks and blood vessel disease.

4. Those who have a family history of strokes or any form of thrombosis to which the pill can make them more susceptible.

5. Women who have psychiatric disorders or bouts of severe depression as the pill may aggravate the condition.

6. Women whose blood group is A, or AB, as they are thought to have a higher risk of thrombosis.

7. Those who have to take some form of daily medicine which may interact with and inactivate the efficacy of the pill. Even taking daily aperients may interfere with absorption, as may other disorders of the alimentary tract.

8. Women who suffer from conditions such as diabetes, epilepsy, cancer, heart disorders, migraine, varicose veins, uterine fibroids, cystic fibrosis, abnormal vaginal bleeding, cystic mastitis, kidney disease, high blood-pressure, jaundice and other liver disorders, certain blood disorders (e.g. leukaemia, sickle cell anaemia, etc.) or have a history of previous thrombosis.

Women also need to know the warning signs of serious complications: swelling of the legs or pain in the legs; shortness of breath; visual disturbances such as blurred vision, seeing flashing lights or problems with contact lenses; severe headaches; unusual chest pain; vague pains in lower abdomen; jaundice.

Conception and the pill

If a woman who is on the pill plans a pregnancy, it is advisable for her to change to another form of contraception at least three months, and preferably six months, before conceiving. This is because:

1. There is a higher risk of congenital abnormalities if conception takes place while the mother is on the pill or her body is still under its influence. It is therefore desirable to be completely back to normal before becoming pregnant.

2. There is a higher incidence of jaundice in the newborn if the mother had been on the pill shortly before conceiving.

The pill is an effective contraceptive. It is easy to take and is aesthetically acceptable. In fact, it can almost be described as the badge of liberated womanhood. Nevertheless, in view of all the many possible associated side-effects and risks, many women are becoming disenchanted with it. And a woman who has a baby entirely dependent on her should seriously consider the wisdom of using it as a long-term method of contraception. But if she does decide to take the pill, and she wishes to breast-feed her baby, then it is advisable to wait until after the puerperium and until the baby is two months old before starting a low-dose pill, as before then it may interfere with the establishment of the milk supply. The effects of the pill on the baby, if any, are not yet known. The mini-pill, however, is the one generally prescribed for lactating mothers.

The argument put forward by those who favour the pill is that nothing in life is without risk. This may be true, but other risks in life are chance ones outside our control, whereas here we do have a choice and can deliberately decide whether to take such risks or not.

Another argument often put forward is that pregnancy is more dangerous than the pill. This is not true. Pregnancy poses little risk to healthy young women. Only those who already have health problems and who would not anyway be eligible for the pill are at higher risk when pregnant. They, however, have the advantage that with good antenatal care, complications can be kept to a minimum or averted, whereas pill-users are often taken unawares by serious complications.

The alternative to the pill is not a baby every year but the choice of a healthier method of contraception which, used conscientiously, can be as effective as the pill.

The IUD

The intra-uterine device (IUD) is an old-fashioned contraceptive which had been discarded for nearly half a century but in the last twenty years it has been up-dated and is now fairly popular. It is a small gadget which can be in any one of a number of different shapes, e.g. loop, coil, T-shape, 7-shape, etc. It is usually made of plastic but it may also be made of metal or a combination of plastic and metal. (For centuries the Arabs used small stones as IUDs to prevent pregnancy in their camels.)

The IUD should be fitted by an experienced doctor. The best time to fit it is during menstruation because the woman is then unlikely to be pregnant and the cervix is softer, making insertion easier. For the same reasons, the puerperium is also a good time for the IUD to be fitted.

After a careful pelvic examination, the doctor will assess the correct size needed which, as a general rule, is the largest size that the woman can tolerate. The straightened IUD, contained in a narrow plastic tube, is inserted through the cervix and is gently nudged into the uterus where it regains its intended shape. One or two nylon threads protrude from the end of the device through the cervix and can be felt high up in the vagina. These threads are used to check that the device is still in place.

Checking for the presence and position of the threads should be done frequently in the first few months, and always after menstruation, to ensure that the IUD is still there, as these are the times when spontaneous expulsion of the IUD can occur. If it does happen then the woman is, of course, not protected and may become pregnant. The way to check is to insert a clean finger in the vagina and to feel for the threads below the cervix. If the IUD is easily expelled then a larger size or a different shape may be needed, providing there are no other adverse symptoms.

The exact contraceptive action of the IUD is not known but it is a foreign body in the uterus and as such is likely to work for any one or a combination of the following reasons:

1. In trying to expel the foreign body inside it, the uterus contracts powerfully and in so doing expels the fertilized egg before implantation can occur.

2. The foreign body in the uterus prevents the cyclical changes in the endometrium (the inside lining of the uterus) which are necessary to make it receptive for implantation.

3. Large white blood cells (phagocytes) may try to destroy the foreign body and indirectly destroy sperm and/or the fertilized egg.

4. The copper in the new IUDs is thought to have a toxic effect on the inner lining of the uterus and/or the fertilized egg.

5. The IUD does not interfere with ovulation or fertilization but causes an early abortion.

It is generally accepted that the plastic IUD can be left inside the uterus indefinitely, while the copper IUD (if the woman is not allergic to the copper) needs to be replaced every two to three years. Nevertheless, all women with an IUD should have an annual gynaecological check-up.

Some authorities believe that prolonged use of the IUD is undesirable. As a foreign body in the uterus, it prevents the complete shedding of the inner uterine lining with menstruation and this may result in undesirable changes in the endometrium. They therefore suggest that the IUD should not be used for more than five years. After that it should be removed and the uterus be given a chance to rest, recover and revert to normal.

Side-effects of the IUD

Not all women can tolerate the IUD. Some have increased and prolonged menstrual bleeding and/or bleeding between periods – as frequently as every week, in one case. The bleeding may be bad enough to cause anaemia and ill-health.

In addition, there may be severe menstrual cramp and constant backache. All these symptoms may settle down within about three months. However, if the bleeding and cramp persist then the IUD will have to be removed. Sometimes a smaller size or different shape may suit better.

Increased vaginal discharge (leucorrhoea) can be an unpleasant side-effect of the IUD. This may be a reaction of the whole genital tract to the irritation of the foreign body in the uterus. The condition should not be ignored but should instead be thoroughly investigated.

Another side-effect is that should there be any inflammation of the cervix, it is prevented from healing by the presence of the threads from the tail of the IUD.

The failure rate of the IUD

The IUD is not always 100 per cent effective and pregnancy has been known to occur even with the IUD still in place. Such a pregnancy may end in spontaneous abortion or it may continue to full term. The IUD itself cannot harm the developing baby as he/she is contained in the amniotic sac (bag of waters) which develops from the fertilized egg, whereas the IUD is in contact with the wall of the uterus and therefore outside the amniotic sac. In these circumstances the doctor may decide to remove the IUD as it can predispose to serious uterine infections. Alternatively, the pregnancy may be allowed to continue to full term:

> After my six-week check-up at the clinic, I had a coil fitted. Having used this device successfully before my pregnancy, it seemed to be a logical contraceptive alternative. However,

several days later, I could not feel the threads (to check that the coil was still in position). I returned to the clinic, and after several rather painful and unsuccessful attempts to locate the elusive device, I was sent for a scan.

The scan showed the presence of the coil, though embedded at the back of the womb. The doctor subsequently informed me that it would still function as a coil. I could have it removed if I wished, but this would involve a minor operation. As I was involved with a new baby at the time, and had been assured as to the safety and efficiency of the device, despite its 'wandering', I opted to leave well alone.

Six months later, as soon as I finished breast-feeding, I fell pregnant again!

I was obviously surprised, and worried about the effect of the coil on the developing foetus. On enquiry, the doctor informed me that they deliver thousands of babies with the coil with no problems at all – a sobering thought! I have gone ahead with this pregnancy, not without anxiety, despite assurances that all will be well. I shall certainly never resort to the coil again.

The woman gave birth, after a two-and-a-half hour drugless labour, to a healthy baby boy who weighed 7 lb 9 oz. But the birth of the baby was not the end of the matter:

Here is the sequel to the coil saga . . . After the delivery of my baby boy (if unplanned, certainly not unwelcome) the placenta was checked for the coil. None could be found. I was assured several times after the birth by doctors and nurses alike that there was absolutely no chance that it could still be present after a delivery. I requested an X-ray or scan, but was again assured that it could not be present, that I must have lost it before conception. I was sure I hadn't.

When my period came three months after the birth, I went to the FPC (family planning clinic) to arrange some other means of contraception. The doctor there, on hearing my tale, said that she would be happier if I had a scan to make sure it was not present as she had had a similar experience with a nurse who had gone through pregnancy and delivery and the coil had stubbornly refused to move. So I went ahead with a scan and X-ray – much to my annoyance yet relief to find someone who took my concern seriously – and there imprinted unmistakeably in glorious celluloid was a bright white bendy piece of totally useless plastic, embedded in the pelvis.

I now have to undergo an operation which could have been performed quite simply after the birth. Instead of which the children have to be looked after for one week while I go into hospital . . .

Here is the final instalment:

I was admitted to hospital on 4 March for a short stay, probably three days . . . . On coming round from my anaesthetic I was greeted by a doctor saying 'Mrs –, Mrs –, we have not found the coil.' I cannot express what I felt! This doctor rang me later on the ward and explained that, because they had been unable to take an X-ray in theatre, they had decided to abandon the operation . . .

The next day, a completely different doctor told me I was fit to go home and that the coil *probably* wouldn't do me any harm! I informed her of three points:

1. I had been told it would still function as a coil and it hadn't. I had become pregnant on it.

2. I had been told it could not possibly still be there after birth and delivery and it was *so*.

3. I was not inclined to believe her when she told me it *probably* wouldn't do me any harm, and that I was not moving from that hospital until the coil had been removed!

I had to wait until the Monday to see the consultant. He informed me that due to an emergency in Casualty the X-ray equipment had not been available and that for my own safety it was better to bring me up to the ward. I couldn't argue with that though I insisted on having an X-ray done then and there with a view to a further attempt at removing it. He grudgingly agreed.

The X-ray proved that in the intervening months since December my coil had moved quite considerably. In the afternoon I was descended upon by the big boss and his retinue. He at least explained everything to me for the first time, and agreed that it would be better if it were removed. He tacked me onto the end of his operating list for the next day with no assurance that he would be able to take me.

I spent a rather fretful day and at 4.30 pm was eventually taken down to theatre for the second time.

This time, when I came round, my husband was sitting next to me holding a small perspex container in his hand. It contained the coil. Never was I more relieved to see anything . . . . Apparently it had been lodged in the fatty tissue around the bowel. They kept me in for an extra day to check that it had not damaged the bowel!!

Complications

As well as the side-effects already described, there are also several serious complications associated with the IUD. These include:

1. The possibility of perforation of the uterine wall. This is more likely to occur when the IUD is first inserted and if there is a scar in the uterus from a previous Caesarean operation. The IUD works its way through the wall of the uterus and into the pelvic cavity where it can cause further complications such as inflammation, adhesions and occasionally intestinal obstruction. Women should never ignore severe abdominal pain when they have an IUD, as it may indicate perforation of the uterus.

2. A greater predisposition to ectopic pregnancy (i.e. the fertilized

egg becomes embedded in the fallopian tube instead of in the uterus) and the danger of shock and haemorrhage when the tube subsequently ruptures.

3. Pelvic infection – a serious complication. The IUD may cause an old infection to flare up or an ascending infection can spread upwards from the vagina, along the threads from the IUD, through the cervix, into the uterus and along the fallopian tubes. Infection of the fallopian tubes (salpingitis) can be responsible for ectopic pregnancies and later infertility. Signs of infection are: raised temperature, vaginal discharge, tenderness low down in the abdomen and painful intercourse.

Contra-indications for the IUD
The IUD is not suitable for women who have:

1. an abnormality of the uterus (or even uterine fibroids);

2. inflammation or infection of any part of the genital tract;

3. menstrual disorders such as painful or heavy periods, or bleeding between periods;

4. certain general conditions such as anaemia; cancer of the cervix or uterus; valvular heart disease (because of the possibility of endocarditis from infection); and any condition requiring anticoagulants as it may lead to greater blood loss and anaemia.

The newer IUDs seem to be better tolerated by women. The expulsion rate is lower and there are fewer side-effects. It is, however, thought that some drugs (e.g. antibiotics, aspirin, etc.) interfere with the effectiveness of the IUD and it may therefore be a wise precaution to use an extra method of contraception when taking such drugs.

The IUD can even be inserted after an act of unprotected intercourse to prevent a pregnancy. The copper IUD is particularly effective in such cases but it has to be inserted within a few days (a maximum of five) of intercourse. Its function then is that of an abortifacient (i.e. it causes an abortion).

The vaginal diaphragm

Placing a barrier between the ovum and the sperm which prevents them coming together is an obvious and simple way of avoiding conception. There are several types of barriers, some for use by women and some for use by men.

Of those designed for use by women, the one most frequently prescribed and easiest to use is the vaginal diaphragm. This is made of soft thin rubber, is dome-shaped, and has a rubber-covered rim which contains a metal spring. It is circular and made in a range of sizes varying from 2-4 inches (5-10cm) in diameter. It is very important to be properly fitted with the correct sized diaphragm by a doctor who is experienced in this work. It also helps if the woman is completely relaxed while being fitted, so that the doctor can easily assess the correct size needed. The diameter of the diaphragm should be the same as the distance from behind the cervix to the pubic bone.

How to insert the diaphragm

Learning to insert the diaphragm correctly is easy if the woman squats and remembers the following guidelines:

1. Lubricating the rim makes insertion easier.

2. Slightly pressing the rim together changes the shape of the diaphragm to make it narrower for easy insertion.

3. To insert the compressed shape into the vagina, guide one end down (towards the floor) and back along the posterior wall of the vagina until it cannot be pushed any further. It is then in the small space behind the cervix (posterior fornix). The front rim of the diaphragm is then pushed firmly up, to rest behind the pubic bone. The diaphragm now covers the cervix and upper part of the vagina and is held in place by the tension of the spring in the rim. The diaphragm can be inserted with the dome either in the up or down position. It is equally effective either way.

4. It is important to check that the diaphragm is correctly in place
   by inserting a finger into the vagina and feeling the hard knob
   of the cervix through the thin rubber. This indicates that the
   cervix is completely covered.

Most women learn to use the diaphragm within a matter of
days, but women who find it difficult can use a special applicator
to insert it.

How to remove the diaphragm

To remove the diaphragm, the woman squats and feels for the rim
in the front and upper part of the vagina, hooks a finger behind the
rim and gives a downward pull, making the whole diaphragm slip
out. It takes practice to be able to use the diaphragm with
confidence and while learning to do so, another method of
contraception should be used in addition.

This may all sound very complicated, but in practice it is not. It
is worth making the effort to learn to use the diaphragm correctly
as it is one of the safest methods of contraception, involves
absolutely no risk to health, and gives rise to no side-effects.
Correctly fitted and correctly used, neither the woman nor her
partner will be aware of it. Nor need it disrupt the spontaneity of
love-making if the woman develops the habit of inserting the
diaphragm every night as part of her bedtime routine.

The diaphragm should be left in place for eight to twelve hours
after intercourse because the sperm in the vagina are still viable for
up to eight hours. So the diaphragm can be removed at lunchtime
the following day. (It can, of course, be removed in the morning if
intercourse did not take place.)

Care of the diaphragm is simple

After removal, the diaphragm is washed with soap and warm (not
hot) water, rinsed, dried carefully to remove all moisture,
checked by holding it against the light to make sure there are no
holes or thin patches in the rubber – especially near the rim – then
lightly powdered with cornflour, potato flour, or talcum powder
(if the woman is not sensitive to the perfume in it) and placed in its

special container until bedtime or when needed.

To enhance the contraceptive effect of the mechanical barrier, the vaginal diaphragm should *always* be used with a spermicidal jelly or cream which also acts as a lubricant when inserting the diaphragm. The jelly or cream is well smeared around the entire rim and a large blob is placed on the upper part of the dome which will be in contact with the cervix. For good measure the lower part of the dome also gets smeared. Thus it becomes a double contraceptive – mechanical as well as chemical.

The spermicidal agent loses its effectiveness after two hours. So if intercourse is delayed for more than two hours after the insertion of the diaphragm, then extra spermicidal cream/jelly should be inserted into the vagina. The same applies if intercourse is repeated: the diaphragm is left in place but extra spermicidal cream/jelly is inserted into the vagina. The diaphragm should be left in until eight to twelve hours after the *last* act of intercourse. If it is not convenient to remove the diaphragm after the recommended eight to twelve hours, it can be left in place in the vagina for as long as 24 hours without any ill-effects. It then needs to be removed and washed before it is inserted again. The diaphragm can be used when the woman is menstruating. If inserted with the dome down, it will hold a fair amount of the menstrual flow, thus making intercourse aesthetically more acceptable.

Failure rate of the diaphragm

The diaphragm needs to be renewed every year. And each time the woman should again be measured internally as the size and shape of the vagina may have altered during the year. A new size may also be needed after childbirth, miscarriage, abortion, gynaecological operations or even if there has been a marked change in body weight:

> When I reached thirty-five... I again used a cap. After using it for over a year I became pregnant – this time accidentally... The doctor at the clinic could only attribute my becoming pregnant to the small failure rate of the cap. The only other reason suggested was that I had lost a little weight just before

becoming pregnant and apparently this can affect the fitting of the cap.

Every woman over the age of 30 years, regardless of her chosen method of contraception, should have an annual gynaecological check-up and a cervical smear to test for cancer (some doctors consider every five years to be adequate). At an annual examination she can also be assessed for a new diaphragm.

Given the right size and used correctly – and again this has to be stressed – the vaginal diaphragm is a healthy and an effective method of contraception. But a pregnancy is likely to result if the diaphragm is: used only sporadically (i.e. if intercourse is sometimes unprotected); carelessly inserted so that the cervix is not covered; used without, or with insufficient, spermicidal agent; removed too soon. In these circumstances failure is due not to the diaphragm but rather to incompetent use of it.

Different types of diaphragm
There are several variations of the vaginal diaphragm. Women who lack good muscle tone, or have certain gynaecological problems, and therefore cannot keep the ordinary diaphragm in place can sometimes be successfully fitted with another type which has a different rim, e.g. *an arcing or bow-bend diaphragm*.

The cervical cap
Another barrier device (and an alternative for women who cannot use a vaginal diaphragm) is the cervical cap. This is thimble-shaped, has a rim, is made of thick rubber or plastic, and is designed to fit over the cervix. The cervical cap also comes in different sizes and the diameter of the lower part of the cervix should equal the diameter of the inside of the rim of the cap. The cap has to be expertly fitted and should only be used on a healthy cervix, i.e. one that is not infected or damaged. The cervical cap is inserted in a similar way to the vaginal diaphragm, but with the dome down. In this case, instead of aiming for the posterior fornix, the cap is pressed together and pushed along the posterior wall of the vagina until it comes to rest against the back of the

cervix. Pressure on the cap is released and it opens. It can then be pushed up to cover the cervix. Again the woman has to check that the cervix is covered by feeling it through the cap. The cervical cap is a little more difficult to insert than the vaginal diaphragm and also requires practice. Sometimes it has a thread for easy removal, or it may be eased off the cervix after first inserting a fingertip inside the cap.

The cervical cap also requires spermicidal cream or jelly, and usually the same general rules apply for its use and care as for the vaginal diaphragm.

The vault cap
Another alternative for women who cannot be fitted with a vaginal diaphragm is the vault cap (dumas). This cap is designed to cover the cervix and 'roof' of the vagina. It is a small, shallow-domed, rubber device and from the thin centre of the shallow dome the rubber gradually thickens towards the rim.

The dumas is also graded in size and also has to be fitted by an experienced doctor. The correct size is the smallest one that will fit evenly into the vault (roof) of the vagina.

The vault cap is inserted with the dome down and in the same way as the cervical cap. When the back of the cap is behind the cervix, the dome is pushed up to cover the cervix, air is expelled and it adheres to the vault of the vagina by suction. It is still necessary to check that the cervix is covered by feeling it through the dome of the cap.

A blob of spermicidal cream or jelly is placed only in the hollow of the dome and is also smeared on the outer part of the cap, but the rim is not treated or lubricated as it would interfere with the suction.

To remove the dumas, the suction is broken by inserting a finger under the rim of the cap and then pulling the cap down and out. The vault cap is used and cared for in the same way as the vaginal diaphragm.

The vimule cap
For women with gynaecological problems who cannot use any of

the above devices, there is the vimule cap. This is designed to incorporate the thimble-shaped dome of the cervical cap to cover the cervix and the thick rubber base of the dumas to keep it in place by suction. The correct size is the smallest one that will fit the cervix and vault of the vagina and this, too, has to be ascertained by an experienced practitioner. Being a combination of the cervical and vault caps, the rules for use, care, and removal are the same as for the others.

The sheath or condom

A barrier device which is used by the man is the sheath or condom (also known by many other names). It is designed to completely cover the erect penis during sexual intercourse. Although there is one standard size to fit all men (about 7½-8 inches or 19-20cm long and about 1½ inches or 4cm in diameter), condoms do vary slightly in other respects:

1. The closed end of the sheath may be either rounded or shaped like a teat.

2. Some come ready lubricated with a spermicide. Those that are not need to be smeared on the outside with spermicidal cream or jelly after being fitted onto the erect penis and before penetrating the vagina.

3. Most are disposable (made of thin but good quality rubber) and meant to be used for only one act of intercourse, but in some countries they are made of sheep intestine, are thicker and can be washed and used again.

4. They are available in a number of different colours or they may be plain.

5. They may be smooth or they may have ridges or other projections for extra vaginal stimulation.

6. If either partner is allergic to rubber, there is a special non-allergic brand available.

7. Though most condoms are full length and are intended to cover the whole erect penis, short condoms are also available. These are designed to cover only the head (glans) of the penis and are known as American or Grecian tips. They are not recommended, as they may slip off or fit too tightly.

Another variation of the sheath is the urethral contraceptive – a small bag to hold the semen with a stem to fit into the man's urethra. This is considered to be harmful and should not be used.

How to use the condom
The condom should always be put on *before* there is any penile contact with the vagina, as the pre-ejaculate secretions often contain live sperm. When fitting the sheath, and to prevent accidental bursting, the air should be expelled from the lower end by compressing the teat or the last half-inch or centimetre of the condom. This space is left free for the semen.

Once the condom has been put on, spermicidal cream or jelly should be smeared on the outside of the sheath. This acts as a lubricant as well as an extra contraceptive.

After orgasm, care must be taken to ensure that the contents of the sheath do not spill into the vagina. For this reason the penis should be withdrawn before the erection has subsided, with the rim of the condom held firmly in place to prevent the device slipping off.

If a condom accidentally bursts during intercourse, then lots of spermicidal cream, jelly or foam should immediately be inserted into the vagina to kill the sperm. Unfortunately, however, this will not affect any sperm that might have entered the cervix at the time of the condom bursting. It is impossible to predict when a condom will burst, but precautions are to ensure that condoms are not used after the expiry date on the packet, or if they look old, or if they have been exposed to light for any length of time as the rubber will have deteriorated.

There are usually two objections to the use of the condom. The first is that couples resent the break in spontaneity of their love-making which fitting the sheath entails. This, however, can be overcome easily if putting on the condom is accepted as part of their sex play. It may in fact help a man who has difficulty in maintaining an erection if his partner undertakes to roll on the condom for him.

The other objection is that the sheath dulls penile sensitivity. This is a disadvantage for some men but it may be an advantage for the man who tends to reach orgasm too quickly as the decreased sensitivity may enable him to delay ejaculation.

Used with care, the condom is an effective contraceptive. It also affords some protection against venereal diseases and genital infections and prevents partners from re-infecting each other while being treated. It is a useful contraceptive after childbirth or miscarriage and before the woman can be fitted with her own barrier device or can resume her preferred method of contraception.[1]

Spermicides

The chemical method of contraception aims to kill the live sperms before they can enter the cervix. The spermicides which do this are available in different forms – either as creams, jellies or aerosol foam which all act immediately, or as suppositories (pessaries) or foaming tablets which both need time (between five and fifteen minutes) to dissolve before they become active. Some of these preparations have special applicators which not only measure the right amount of spermicide to deal with one ejaculation but also make it easier to deposit it at the top of the vagina and near to the entrance of the cervix. There is also a spermicide in the form of a water-soluble plastic film designed to cover the cervix, but it is thought that this sometimes begins to melt before it covers the cervix and the main concentration is therefore not where it should be.

[1] The creams normally prescribed for treating the fungus infection monilia destroy rubber. They should therefore not be used if the diaphragm or sheath is being used.

Although the aerosol foam is also thought to trap the sperm and act as a physical barrier, the chemical contraceptives are not considered to be wholly reliable on their own. This is because of the following practical difficulties: foaming tablets need moisture to dissolve and if there is not enough moisture (lubrication) then they may not dissolve completely; body heat tends to melt the jelly and make it more likely to drip out of the vagina; suppositories dissolve slowly in one place and may not distribute the spermicide as well as they are meant to; if the product is old, it may no longer be spermicidal. All chemical products deteriorate and lose potency with time.

Even if the product is fresh, each dose of spermicide has only a limited time of potency (one to two hours) and should be inserted into the vagina just before intercourse. If intercourse is delayed or repeated, then more spermicide should be used.

If one particular spermicide irritates either partner then another make or preparation may be better tolerated – it sometimes needs a little experimenting to find the product that suits best.

Spermicides are particularly good if used in conjunction with a mechanical barrier, e.g. aerosol foam with the condom, creams and jellies with the vaginal diaphragm or cervical cap. The others can be used with any of the devices. The creams and jellies also act as a lubricant and facilitate the insertion or application of the barrier devices. Used correctly the combined chemical and mechanical contraceptive effects are very high.

Post-coital or 'morning after' contraception

This type of contraception aims to prevent implantation of the fertilized egg after unprotected intercourse or the accidental bursting of the sheath. It is an emergency treatment only and should not be regarded as a regular method of contraception, mainly because of the high level of hormones involved.

The present favoured method of administration is an initial high dose of certain combined contraceptive pills and these are repeated twelve hours later. This is the Yuzpe method and even though it is considered to be effective if started within 72 hours after intercourse, it is best to start treatment as soon as possible, e.g. within twelve to 24 hours, especially if it coincides with the time of ovulation. Nausea and vomiting are likely side-effects but if the vomiting is severe then it should be reported to the doctor.

Another way of preventing implantation of the fertilized egg is to have an IUD inserted within five days after unprotected intercourse.

Long-lasting steroid contraceptives

These can be given in the form of tablets, injections or implants. The contraceptive effect lasts from one to six months (depending on the product used) and the newer slow-releasing implants are meant to be effective for one year.

These preparations contain much higher doses of the same hormones as are contained in the contraceptive pills and side-effects are therefore liable to be the same. In addition, quite severe menstrual disturbances have also been reported.

If side-effects occur, it may be possible to remove an implant but if the contraceptive was in the form of a tablet or injection, then it will be impossible to stop any side-effects while the drug remains potent. For the woman concerned, this can be a lengthy time of misery.

High doses of these powerful drugs are also thought by some authorities to be associated with risks of cancer and subsequent infertility.

Long-lasting contraceptives are therefore not to be recommended and women should beware of them, especially as they have sometimes been administered (after an abortion or childbirth) without the woman's knowledge or consent.

'Natural' methods

In view of all the potential risks, side-effects, and complications associated with so many contraceptives, the idea of a 'natural' method is becoming increasingly more appealing for many couples. But these methods, too, are not without some dis-advantages and problems.

Abstinence

Abstaining from intercourse is one obvious and foolproof way of avoiding conception. It does, of course, frustrate the sexual purpose of the partnership and so, as a long-term method, is neither practical nor desirable. It can, however, be managed on odd occasions or for short spells. Abstaining from intercourse need not rule out other forms of sexual activity, provided that the couple carefully avoid any contact of the penis with the vagina, as sperm contained in the pre-ejaculation secretions are capable of moving up from the entrance of the vagina to cause a pregnancy.

Coitus interruptus

This involves withdrawing the penis from the vagina just before orgasm and ejaculating the semen (containing sperm) outside and away from the vagina. This method requires control and good timing from the man, and the possibility of misjudgement can be a source of anxiety for the woman as well. Also, if withdrawal takes place before the woman has reached orgasm, she will be left dissatisfied and tense, so the method is not free from emotional strain. There is also the risk of live sperm being present in the penile secretion even before ejaculation. This is not really a satisfactory or completely reliable method of contraception. Nevertheless, it is better than no protection at all on the odd occasion, but its disadvantages should be realized.

The 'rhythm' method

All the 'natural' methods of contraception practised by women are based on the principle of avoiding sexual intercourse during the woman's fertile phase of the menstrual cycle. The rhythm (safe period) method relies on avoiding intercourse at the time of ovulation, when there will be a ripe ovum in the fallopian tube ready to be fertilized. Ovulation generally occurs fourteen days before menstruation begins. This applies to irregular, long, and short menstrual cycles, as well as to regular cycles. In regular cycles the time of ovulation can be anticipated fairly accurately. But even in a regular 28-day cycle allowance must still be made for a margin of error – believed to be two to three days either way.

It is relatively easy to calculate the safe period if the woman has a perfect 28-day cycle. Count back fifteen days from the first day of the next expected onset of menstruation and this is the day of ovulation. Allow two days before and two days after day 14 and the safe period will be eleven days from the first day of the last menstrual period and twelve days before the next period. But another factor has to be taken into account: if intercourse has taken place on day 10 and the woman ovulates the next day, there may still be live sperm around to fertilize an egg which has been released early. Similarly, an egg may still be fertilized if intercourse takes place on day 17. Therefore, another two days should be allowed at each end of the unsafe period for either possibility. The safe phase is now whittled down to nine days from the first day of the last period (four to five days of these being menstruation) and the ten days before the next menstruation. Many gynaecologists suggest that another day should be deducted from either end for good measure, thus reducing the 'safe' period even further (see Table 1, p.100).

So if you have, and always have had, a regular 28-day cycle without any variation at all, and if you and your partner's sexual desires coincide exactly with the safe days and nights, then the rhythm method is likely to work for you.

But relatively few women have a perfect 28-day cycle and even those who do may find that it can change for various reasons such as physical and/or emotional stress, severe dieting, illness, anaemia, travel, change of job and various body disturbances. Menstrual cycles between 21 and 35 days are considered normal and the actual duration of a normal period can be between three and seven days.

It is still possible for women who have irregular cycles to use the rhythm method of contraception, but in a slightly different way. To calculate the safe period, keep a careful record of nine to twelve (the more the better) consecutive menstruations, noting the longest and the shortest cycles. Each cycle is calculated from the first day of the menstrual period to the day before the onset (first day) of the next period. Having recorded the nine to twelve cycles, now pick out the longest and the shortest ones. From the shortest cycle deduct eighteen and from the longest cycle deduct eleven (this is a standard formula). Example: If the shortest cycle was 21 days, deduct eighteen and the result is three, i.e. day three becomes the first unsafe day. If the longest cycle was 31 days, deduct eleven and the result is 20, i.e. day 20 becomes the last unsafe day. The safe phase is therefore days one and two of the cycle and from day 21 until menstruation begins again – which means that only days 1 and 2 of the menstrual period are safe and then there is a long wait until day 21 for the rest of the safe phase. Avoiding intercourse for more than two weeks in every cycle (as in the above case) can throw great strain on a couple and only the highly motivated are likely to persevere for any length of time with the rhythm method.

Calculating the 'safe period', based on a 28-day cycle

Table 1

Day

1	menstruation	safe period
2	menstruation	safe period
3	menstruation	safe period
4	menstruation	safe period
5	menstruation	safe period
6		safe period
7		safe period
8		safe period
9	for good measure	
10	to ensure live sperm are not still present	
11	to ensure live sperm are not still present	
12	margin of error	
13	margin of error	
14	OVULATION	
15	margin of error	

16	margin of error	
17	to ensure egg is still not fertilizable	
18	to ensure egg is still not fertilizable	
19	for good measure	
20		safe period
21		safe period
22		safe period
23		safe period
24		safe period
25		safe period
26		safe period
27		safe period
28		safe period
1	menstruation	safe period

The temperature method

This method involves recording the basal body temperature (BBT, i.e. the temperature of the body at rest) every morning. The time of ovulation cannot be predicted but immediately after it occurs there is a rise in body temperature of about ½-1°Fahrenheit. After ovulation, the high level of progesterone from the corpus luteum (see p.71) keeps the body temperature raised. So if intercourse is avoided on the first day of raised temperature and the two following days of raised temperature (to ensure that the ovum is no longer fertilizable), plus another day just to be absolutely sure, then the rest of the cycle is safe.

Great care must be taken over recording the temperature. As it is the BBT which is significant, it should be taken immediately on waking in the morning and before any kind of activity such as talking, getting up to empty the bladder, cleaning teeth, sipping water or tea, or even shaking down the thermometer. This should be done the day before and the thermometer placed ready for use in the morning. Your partner can help by handing you the thermometer as soon as you wake. It is advisable to keep the thermometer in your mouth for at least five minutes.

Apart from the strong motivation needed to accept the

tediousness of this method, there are two other main disadvantages: any infection or mild illness with a slight rise in temperature may give a false reading; there is no indication of the safe phase before ovulation, so intercourse has to be avoided from the beginning of the cycle and until three days after ovulation.

To overcome the latter disadvantage, it is possible to combine the rhythm method and the temperature method. Before ovulation the safe phase is calculated by the rhythm method, and then the temperature method is used to establish the exact time of ovulation.

The cervical mucus method (Billings Method)

This method is based on the ability to recognize the following changes which occur in the mucus secreted from the cervix throughout the menstrual cycle:

1. After menstruation the cervical mucus is thick, viscid, and constitutes a physical barrier which traps the sperm, and thus prevents them from moving into the uterus and through the uterus to the fallopian tubes. As there is little or no discharge at this time, this phase is known as 'dry days'.

2. As the cycle progresses and the oestrogen level rises with the maturation of the graafian follicles (see p.71), the cervical mucus gradually liquifies and becomes thinner and more stretchy. Sperm can now swim through the cervix and uterus to the fallopian tubes, making this an unsafe phase known as 'wet days'.

3. With ovulation (maybe a day or two before and after ovulation) the cervical mucus becomes an almost clear, profuse, slippery discharge. The mucus can be stretched between forefinger and thumb without breaking (spinnbarkeit) and resembles the white of egg. This, of course, is the most fertile phase and is therefore unsafe for intercourse if the couple do not want to conceive.

4. After ovulation and under the influence of progesterone from

the corpus luteum, the cervical mucus gradually returns to its non-receptive state for sperm. It becomes a thick, gelatinous, tenacious and impenetrable plug again. The safe phase is *after* the three days that follow the day of maximum 'wetness'.

These are the general principles but they may not always be as clearly defined as this. This method requires tuition from an experienced person who can interpret individual variations of the cervical mucus, and even then practice and experience is needed before a woman becomes confident about using this method of avoiding unwanted pregnancies. Cervical and vaginal infections can mask true readings and some medication (e.g. cortisone) may simulate the action of oestrogen and affect the cervical mucus. Also, previous cautery of the cervix may have damaged the cervical crypts and glands that secrete the cervical mucus.

The sympto-thermal method

This is a combination of the cervical mucus method and the temperature method. In the early phase of the cycle the mucus is used as a guide to establish the onset of the ovulatory phase (the fertile period). After that the BBT is used to establish the exact time of ovulation and the beginning of the infertile phase, i.e. after three to four days of raised temperature.

Other signs of ovulation

Apart from the changes in the cervical mucus, the cervix itself undergoes recognizable changes throughout the cycle. After menstruation the cervix feels hard and the opening into the vagina (external os) is closed. Gradually, as the cycle progresses, it loosens up and at about the time of ovulation it feels soft and the opening actually gapes slightly. After ovulation it returns to its firm, closed state.

The colour of the cervix also changes; it is light pink at the time of ovulation and gets slightly darker in colour as the cycle progresses towards menstruation, when it is dark pink.

Most women are completely unaware of the time of ovulation but some experience quite acute lower abdominal pain *(mittelschmerz)* in the middle of the cycle. This pain has on occasion been diagnosed as acute appendicitis but at the time of operation it was found that no pathology existed and ovulation only had occurred.

Abdominal cramping at any time, as well as in mid-cycle, may be associated with the bowel or other internal organs and should not automatically be assumed to be due to ovulation, so it cannot always be used as a guide to the fertile phase. Some women experience low back-pain in the middle of the cycle and this, too, should not automatically be assumed to coincide with ovulation.

Another relatively rare symptom which may or may not be associated with ovulation is spotting or a slight bloody discharge from the vagina in the middle of the cycle. Before it is assumed to be, and used as, a guide to ovulation, the woman should be checked by a gynaecologist to eliminate more serious causes of bleeding. All these symptoms are probably due to the high level of oestrogen prior to ovulation, but they need to be further evaluated before they are used as definite signs of ovulation. It again needs to be stressed that the cycle can be affected by illness, travel, emotional upsets, post-partum and lactation.

Although the fertile phase of the menstrual cycle is normally round about the time of ovulation, nevertheless it has been known for young women under the age of 35 to ovulate spontaneously when making love or having an orgasm. This is the reason why the so-called 'safe period' is not always safe. Ovulation may even occur during menstruation but there is doubt as to whether the fertilized egg can become embedded if the uterine lining is being shed.

Abortion

Once a fertilized egg has become firmly embedded in the lining of the uterus, it is not easy to dislodge it. It requires active interference in the form of an abortion to loosen it from the wall of the uterus and to remove it. The techniques used to do so depend on the length of the pregnancy and the method favoured by the doctor.

Vacuum aspiration

In the first three months of a pregnancy the most popular procedure is vacuum aspiration. This can be done either under a general anaesthetic or a local anaesthetic. The cervical canal is dilated to allow a tube (cannula) to be inserted. Negative pressure through the cannula is gradually built up from a vacuum pump and the contents of the uterus sucked or vacuumed out. In the first six weeks of a pregnancy (i.e. within two weeks of the first missed menstrual period) this same procedure can be done with or without a local anaesthetic and is known as *menstrual regulation*, because there may not yet be proof of a pregnancy.

Dilation and curettage (D & C)

Another way to empty the uterus in the first three months of pregnancy is by dilation and curettage (D & C) under a general anaesthetic. The cervix has to be dilated more than for a vacuum aspiration to allow for an instrument (curette) to be inserted. The curette is used to scrape off and remove the foetus and placenta from the wall of the uterus.

After three months gestation, it becomes increasingly difficult and dangerous to empty the uterus because risk of complications is greater. The uterus is larger and more vascular (i.e. has an increased blood supply). The lining of the uterus is more spongy and the walls are thinner. The placenta is fully formed and effectively anchors a larger foetus securely inside the uterus.

Dilatation and evacuation (D & E)

The present trend of procuring late abortions is by dilatation and evacuation (D & E). The cervix is dilated to about 5 cm, either with metal dilators or a prostaglandin (hormone-like) pessary placed in contact with the cervix, or by inserting into the cervix a sea plant (laminaria) which expands when in contact with moisture. Once the cervix is sufficiently dilated, the membranes are ruptured and the foetus and placenta removed with a special type of forceps. Very often the uterus is vacuumed or curetted afterwards to ensure that nothing has been left behind. This procedure is usually done after giving a paracervical block, i.e. injecting a local anaesthetic around the cervix. It may also be done under general anaesthesia.

Aminiocentesis

Another method of inducing a late abortion is by amniocentesis, which involves removing some of the amniotic fluid around the foetus and replacing it with either a strong solution of salt, or prostaglandin. This is done under a local anaesthetic and through the abdominal wall. The salt solution damages the placenta and kills the foetus. After some time (within 36 hours) the uterus starts contracting and so expels its contents in the same way as it does in a full-term labour.

Hysterotomy

The foetus and placenta can also be removed through a hysterotomy (mini-caesar) between three and six months of pregnancy (this is not to be confused with hysterectomy which is the removal of the uterus). A hysterotomy involves a cut in the uterus through the abdomen, usually under a general anaesthetic. It can also be done through the vagina but this procedure is even more hazardous. A hysterotomy carries a higher risk of death than any other method of abortion.

Therapeutic abortions

When the pregnant state constitutes a hazard to a woman's life or health, then she will be advised to have her pregnancy terminated by having a therapeutic abortion.

There are relatively few conditions which jeopardize the physical health of a pregnant woman. The main ones are:

some (but not all) forms of heart disease, kidney disease and lung disease;
some (but not all) disorders of the blood and metabolism;
some (but not all) types of cancer.

Women whose emotional and/or mental health is likely to be harmed by the continuation of a pregnancy are those who are victims of rape or incest, or those who suffer from some forms of psychiatric illness. Abortions for social reasons and 'abortions on demand' tend to be included in this category.

Pregnant women whose babies are likely to be physically or mentally damaged are also candidates for therapeutic abortions, if they wish it. These include women who, in the first twelve to fourteen weeks of pregnancy, had German measles, viral hepatitis or other virus infections which are implicated in damaging the developing embryo; women whose foetus has some genetic or chromosomal abnormality, ascertained from either a blood test, or an ultrasound scan, or an amniocentesis. Amniocentesis involves examining foetal cells from a sample of the amniotic fluid in which the baby is developing.

Possible complications
All abortions are potentially dangerous, even when done by an experienced doctor under ideal conditions. Risks of complications are much greater if abortions are done by an unqualified person, and women should *never* attempt to abort themselves. Risks of complications also increase as the pregnancy becomes more established. Complications vary according to the method of abortion and, apart from those associated with anaesthetics, include the following:

1. Perforation of uterine wall by curette or canulla. This may heal on its own or may require a repair operation under general anaesthesia. Sometimes the perforation involves damage to the bowel.

2. If all products of the pregnancy have not been removed and the abortion has been incomplete, then another D & C becomes necessary.

3. Haemorrhage can lead to death unless bleeding is stopped promptly and the lost blood replaced with transfusions.

4. Pelvic infection may spread to the fallopian tubes causing infertility or subsequent ectopic (tube) pregnancies.

5. Damage to the cervix may lead to the inability to carry a

subsequent pregnancy to full term. Such an 'incompetent cervix' leads to repeated late miscarriages or to premature labours, but future pregnancies can be helped by a technique known as Shirodkar Stitch (see p.24).

6. Embolism, i.e. a foreign substance such as air, blood clot, etc., which inadvertently enters the circulation through the dilated blood vessels in the lining of the uterus. This is a dangerous complication which can result in sudden death.

7. Rhesus-negative women are at risk of developing antibodies if blood from a Rhesus-positive foetus enters the woman's circulation. All such women should be protected with an injection of anti-D gamma globulin within 72 hours of the abortion.

8. The scar from the cut of a hysterotomy constitutes a permanent weakness in the uterine wall and may predispose to the need for Caesarean deliveries of subsequent full-term babies.

9. Damage to the endometrium may result in a retained placenta in a subsequent labour with danger of haemorrhage, shock and the need for a manual removal under general anaesthesia.

10. A tendency to miscarry subsequent wanted babies.

Emotional reactions vary according to the woman's circumstances. Women who desperately wanted an abortion will be greatly relieved. Those who wanted the baby but had abortions for medical or social reasons are more likely to be upset or depressed or regret it. Many women, even if they originally wanted the abortion, feel guilty for years after the event. A late abortion is more upsetting for a woman than an early one.

Abortion is not as harmless a procedure as women sometimes imagine, or are led to believe it to be; there are associated dangers. It should not be considered as a convenient method of birth control and undertaken lightly, instead healthier methods of contraception should be chosen and practised. Oddly enough, most women who seek abortions are those who had unprotected intercourse rather than failed contraception.

Sterilization

Sterilization is not a method of contraception but the permanent ending of the ability to reproduce. It can be the logical solution for the woman who suffers from some disabling disease and whose life could be threatened by the strain of a pregnancy and labour, or for the person who is a carrier of some hereditary disease that cannot as yet be cured. It is not meant for the young and the healthy who just want to avoid pregnancy.

Female sterilization

Both men and women can be sterilized. Female sterilization involves damaging the fallopian tubes to prevent the egg from meeting the sperm. This is achieved by any of the following means:

1. Cutting out a small portion from each of the two fallopian tubes. The cut ends are then tied off and sometimes the end near the uterus is stitched to it.

2. Cutting off the fimbriated end (the end near the ovary) of each fallopian tube.

3. Burning each tube with an electric cautery.

4. Closing the fallopian tubes with metal clips or plastic rings. This method is meant to be reversible.

Female sterilization is usually done under a general anaesthetic but some methods can also be done under a local anaesthetic. Most operations are done through the abdomen and involve either one or two small cuts below the navel, or a small cut above the pubic hair line (though sometimes the cut can be long, even stretching from the navel to the pubic bone).

It is also possible to reach the fallopian tubes through a cut in the vagina and behind the cervix. This is not a popular method as it is more difficult to do and there is also greater risk of infection from the vaginal bacteria. A new approach is through a special telescopic instrument which is inserted into the vagina and passed through the cervix and into the uterus. The fallopian tubes are then cauterized where they enter the upper part of the uterus.

Damaging the fallopian tubes only makes conception impossible; it does not affect the woman's other reproductive functioning. Her ovaries still produce eggs which disintegrate and are absorbed. She can still menstruate and her hormone production remains normal. Her sexual response and behaviour is unaffected; in fact, it may improve considerably once the fear of pregnancy is removed.

Male sterilization

The principle of male sterilization is to stop the live sperm from reaching the penis. Live sperm are produced in the two testicles contained in the scrotum and this function is controlled by the follicle-stimulating hormone (FSH) from the pituitary gland. From each testicle a tube (the vas deferens) leads, through the prostate gland, to the urethra. As the sperm are propelled along the vas deferens they continue to mature, become vigorous and capable of fertilizing the ovum.

To interrupt the sperms' journey requires a small operation (vasectomy) which although usually done under a local anaesthetic, may also be done under a general anaesthetic. A small portion of each vas deferens is removed and the cut ends are tied off. This can be done through one central cut in the scrotum or two cuts (one for each vas) on either side of the scrotum.

As there are still many millions of live sperm in the part of the vas above the cut portion, the man continues to be fertile until all these have been ejaculated and this may take up to twenty acts of intercourse. It is therefore important that some form of contraception is used until at least two semen specimens are free of sperm.

A vasectomy does not change the man's sexuality nor his sexual functioning. It only affects his fertility. A man's masculinity is controlled by the hormone testosterone which is secreted by the testicles under the influence of the luteinizing hormone (LH) of the pituitary gland and passed directly into the blood stream. Even the seminal fluid remains the same (apart from the absence of live sperm) as it is produced by the two seminal vesicles, the prostate gland and the two bulbo-urethral glands. A vasectomy is not the same as castration, which involves the destruction or removal of the testicles and therefore the source of testosterone.

Sterilization should be accepted as irreversible, and should therefore not be undertaken lightly. It is unlikely that a man or a woman will be aware of any physical effects of the operation (apart from sterility). But some men and women are affected emotionally and this can lead to anxiety states, depression and sexual problems such as female sexual apathy and male impotence.

The other major consideration is that no one can predict what life has in store. A child can die through an accident or illness. That particular child can, of course, never be replaced but another pregnancy and a new baby can give hope, distraction and positive direction to the grieving parents. Then there is the possibility of losing a partner either through divorce or death. In the event of a new relationship at a later date, there may be a wish for a child. Great tragedies have befallen people in fire, car, sea, train, and plane accidents when more than one member of a family has perished.

In such circumstances sterilization can be bitterly regretted and a reversal sought. Although it may sometimes be possible to re-align the fallopian tubes or the vas deferens, restoring fertility is not often achieved and this can cause great unhappiness.

Another point about sterilization, as with all surgical procedures, is that there is always risk of complications such as bleeding, infections, etc. An added male complication is the development of sperm antibodies. The testicles continue to manufacture live sperm but as the sperm cannot move along the cut vas, they are absorbed into the circulation. They are in fact foreign bodies in the blood and antibodies are created to destroy them. Some authorities believe that this auto-immune response may have some adverse effects in years to come.

Is it possible to choose the sex of the baby?

The baby's sex is determined at conception and depends on the chromosome content of the particular sperm which fertilizes the ripe ovum.

The testicles produce roughly equal numbers of X-chromosome sperm (gynosperm) and Y-chromosome sperm (androsperm), whereas ova carry only the X-chromosome. When an X-sperm fertilizes the ovum, the result is XX and becomes a female embryo; when a Y-sperm fertilizes the ovum, the result is XY and will be a male embryo.

Chromosomes are thread-like structures and each chromosome carries hundreds of genes. The gene is the unit of DNA (deoxyribonucleic acid) responsible for characteristics inherited not only from the parents but also from generations of past ancestors.

The human being is made up of millions of living cells. The cells vary widely in their structure and function but each cell has a nucleus which contains 23 pairs of chromosomes, i.e. a total of 46.

When body cells reproduce themselves (for growth and repair), they split into two halves (mitosis) and each half is therefore an exact replica of the original cell – this includes the chromosomes which split lengthwise. But this does not happen to the sex cells – the ovum and the sperm – which during their formation undergo special divisions that in fact actually halve their chromosome content (meiosis) so that the mature ovum and the mature sperm each contains only 23 chromosomes. Thus, at conception when the sperm fuses with the ovum, the zygote (fertilized egg) gets the full number of 46 chromosomes – 23 from the mother and 23 from the father and so inherits equally from each parent.

The variety of combination of genes in the chromosomes is infinite and so the resulting baby becomes unique and quite unlike any other individual, even though there may be recognizable inherited characteristics, mannerisms and looks specific to either the mother's or the father's families.

It has been suggested that the X-sperm and the Y-sperm also differ physiologically in certain other ways:

1. The Y-sperm is round-headed, smaller and moves faster than the larger, oval-headed X-sperm.

2. The Y-sperm is more frail than the X-sperm which is stronger and also lives longer. (The Y-sperm lives about 24 hours whereas the X-sperm lives about two to three days. The ovum lives 12 to 24 hours.)

3. Both types of sperm favour an alkaline medium. If the environment is slightly acid then the frail Y-sperm is less likely to survive, whereas the tougher X-sperm may well do so.

If all this is correct (and there is by no means general agreement about this) then by making use of these factors, a couple should be able to influence the sex of the baby as follows:

To conceive a boy

1. The couple should avoid intercourse until ovulation occurs, then the faster moving Y-sperm are more likely to reach the ovum first. If they make love just prior to ovulation, then the tougher and longer-living X-sperm will still be around and one is likely to fertilize the ovum before the Y-sperm arrive. Abstaining from intercourse until ovulation occurs will also ensure maximum sperm count which favours the Y-sperm.

2. Deep penetration when ejaculating will deposit the sperm at the opening of the cervix and make the journey of the sperm shorter. The cervical mucus tends to be alkaline, thus giving the Y-sperm a favourable environment.

To conceive a girl

1. The couple should make love normally but avoid the actual time of ovulation. Intercourse should be stopped two to three days before ovulation so that when ovulation occurs the Y-sperm will no longer be viable but the longer-living X-sperm

are still around to fertilize the ovum. X-sperm are more likely to survive in a low sperm count.

2. The man should avoid deep penetration when ejaculating as the vagina is normally acid and will favour the survival of the tougher X-sperm and eliminate the Y-sperm.

Douching to create an acid or an alkaline environment for the favoured sperm is not recommended for the following reasons:

1. It is possible to damage the sperm by too strong a solution.

2. The solution may irritate the vaginal tissues.

3. Washing out or damaging the protective vaginal flora predisposes the vagina to infestation with foreign bacteria.

Diet Theory

Another theory about sex determination before conception is a dietary one. It has been suggested that a diet rich in potassium and sodium favours the Y-sperm and will result in a boy, whereas a diet rich in calcium and magnesium favours the X-sperm and will result in a girl. It seems that both parents have to adhere to the diet for six weeks prior to conception. Success of over 70 per cent is claimed for this method by one Paris clinic. If you are interested in trying this method, do get professional guidance for a diet from a nutritionist or sympathetic doctor to avoid imbalance or deficiencies of other essential nutrients.[1]

[1] I have no personal knowledge of the effectiveness of the dietary method but know many couples who claim to have used the other method successfully.

Is it possible to become infertile after having had a child?

Causes of infertility are diverse and numerous. It is possible for problems which can interfere with conception to arise at any time, even after a couple have had one or more successful pregnancies. Another factor is that as women get older they become marginally less fertile. It is said that a woman is most fertile between the ages of sixteen and 25 years. After that fertility gradually begins to decline but mostly age is not, on its own, significant or a cause of infertility (except, of course, after the menopause). The father's testicles provide about two hundred million sperm in one ejaculation to fertilize one egg. These sperm have to make the long and tortuous journey from the epididymis (where they are stored), along the vas deferens, through the prostate gland (where secretions from the seminal vesicles and the prostate gland are added to make up the seminal fluid which keeps the sperm alive and active), along the penile urethra, into the vagina, through the cervix, through the uterus, along the fallopian tubes to meet the ovum – and then only one sperm will fertilize the egg.

Difficulties associated with sperm

Obstacles can occur, and progress can be halted, in any of the following ways:

1. The testicles may not produce enough sperm.

2. There may be too few healthy sperm.

3. Any constriction in the vas deferens will prevent the sperm from getting through.

4. The prostate gland may be unhealthy or inactive and the seminal fluid may fail to keep the sperm alive.

5. There may be problems with ejaculation.

6. Once in the vagina, the environment may be too acid and so kill the sperm.

7. The cervical mucus may be too thick for the sperm to penetrate so that they become enmeshed in it and can go no further.

8. The fallopian tubes may be blocked, preventing the sperm from getting through.

9. The sperm may reach the fallopian tubes safely and not find an egg to fertilize.

The mother's essential contribution to conception is to produce one ripe ovum every month, to have fallopian tubes that function normally, to have a healthy uterus where the fertilized egg can grow into a full-term baby and as already mentioned elsewhere, the pH (i.e. the level of acidity and alkalinity) in the vagina and the cervix must be favourable for the sperm to survive.

These few and simple requirements can still present great difficulties for many women. Regular ovulation depends, in addition to healthy ovaries, on normal functioning of the pituitary, thyroid and adrenal glands as well as the hypothalamus. Blocked fallopian tubes result mainly from infections but may also be due to spasm or kinking. The uterine lining may not be receptive because of disease. Unfavourable vaginal and cervical mucus results from any of the many infections to which these parts are prone, or some chemical lubricants.

Fertilization takes place in one or other of the fallopian tubes. From the millions of ejaculated sperm only a few thousand manage to reach the fallopian tubes. They surround the ripe ovum but only one will fertilize it. The fertilized egg then grows by the process of cell division (mitosis) and gets wafted along the fallopian tube to the uterus. It will embed in the already prepared spongy uterine lining and here it will be safe for its nine months of intra-uterine growth.

Difficulties associated with the egg

Simple though the aim is, the zygote (fertilized egg), too, may encounter problems:

1. There may be a partial blockage in the fallopian tube which allows the sperm to squirm through but not the zygote, or tubal function may be faulty and the zygote does not get wafted along to the uterus. Both conditions result in an ectopic pregnancy with the associated risks of rupture of the tube, haemorrhage, shock and loss of pregnancy.

2. The uterine lining may be diseased and the zygote cannot implant.

3. The zygote may implant but the hormone support (progesterone) is inadequate to maintain the pregnancy and the zygote gets expelled from the uterus as a miscarriage.

In addition to all these obvious causes, there are many other factors which directly or indirectly contribute towards a couple's infertility.

Nutrition

It is now believed that diets deficient in many nutrients, particularly vitamin E, folic acid, iron and zinc, can affect fertility in both men and women. An extreme example is the woman suffering from anorexia nervosa who has stopped menstruating and ovulating.

Drugs

Not only heavy smoking, too much alcohol and drug abuse, but also some tranquillizers and drugs prescribed as medicines can affect fertility by inhibiting ovulation and sperm production. One such example is the contraceptive pill which can over-suppress ovarian function and result in 'post-pill infertility'.

Psychological stress

Tension, anxiety, urgency and other emotional stress can disrupt the normal hypothalamic-pituitary functioning and interfere with the production of sperm and ova; can cause spasm in the fallopian tubes and vas deferens and thus prevent the meeting of sperm and egg; may also cause sexual problems. Fatigue can reduce the sperm count.

Sperm antibodies

Both men and women can develop antibodies which destroy sperm. Some women's bodies react to sperm in the genital tract by creating antibodies to destroy them. In men, it is a form of auto-immunity, and the antibodies created destroy the body's own sperm. Neither condition is very common.

Sexual problems

Painful intercourse, vaginismus (involuntary spasms of the lower part of the vagina), impotence (failure to achieve or to maintain an erection) and ejaculatory difficulties may all be responsible for the inability to conceive.

Infections

Fertility in men can be temporarily reduced during and shortly after an illness with a high temperature or by some debilitating illness like tuberculosis. An attack of mumps after puberty which involves the testes may impair their normal functioning. Vaginal and cervical infections can kill sperm. Infections from an intra-uterine device can scar, damage or block the fallopian tubes. Most damage, however, is done by sexually-transmitted infections which are not treated promptly. A common culprit is gonorrhoea (see p.36) but other pelvic infections can also spread to and block the fallopian tubes and seminal ducts.

Congenital abnormalities

Congenital abnormalities or defective development of any of the genital organs in the man or the woman are primary causes of infertility and do not apply to the couple who have already conceived. For them only the secondary causes of infertility apply.

How to encourage successful conception

Many problems of infertility require medical help and some are, as yet, insoluble. Nevertheless, there are several simple things that a couple who wish to have a baby can themselves do to encourage successful conception.

Diet
Optimum health in the partners is an obvious advantage. Changing to a wholesome and well-mixed diet will provide them with all the nutrients, vitamins and trace elements their bodies need to function normally, as well as correct any tendency to anaemia. Vitamin E has been described as the fertility vitamin and it can be taken safely as a supplement of 200-300 international units daily by the woman as well as the man.

Relaxation
Learning to relax, physically and emotionally, and developing a calm state of mind will ensure that conception is not being inhibited emotionally. That this is a factor is often demonstrated when a couple conceive after adopting a baby or even when making arrangements to adopt. There is a valid physiological explanation for this, and it applies equally to both partners. The production of pituitary hormones for ovulation and mature sperm is controlled by releasing factors from the hypothalamus in the brain. The hypothalamus is sensitive to and liable to be effected by anxiety or emotional distress and sustained emotions can disrupt the hypothalamic-pituitary interaction. It is one example of how the state of mind can affect the internal body functioning.

We had decided that we would like to start a family in December and so I came off the pill . . . By March, nothing had happened and a promotion unexpectedly came my way so we decided to postpone a 'little one'. The very next month I conceived. It has been quite fascinating talking to other mothers who have experienced very similar experiences (i.e. the more you try, the harder it appears to be).

Visualization exercises

As it is believed that quite a number of infertility cases are due to psychosomatic causes, it may be worthwhile for both partners to direct their minds positively by practising a simple exercise in *visualizing* successful conception, as follows:

1. Sit in a comfortable chair.

2. Relax all voluntary muscles.

3. Close your eyes and reach a calm state of mind.

4. Consciously slow down your breathing.

5. The woman visualizes the whole process of conception, from the depositing of sperm high up in the vagina and their journey to the fallopian tube, the meeting and fertilizing of the ovum, and the journey of the fertilized egg along the fallopian tube to the uterus where it embeds. At the same time she visualizes all her organs as healthy and functioning normally. (There is no need to aim for physiological accuracy, just visualize the process as you understand it and correct and normalize whatever you consider to be the problem in your mind's eye.)

6. The man visualizes the healthy testicles producing millions of active sperm and their normal and effortless journey to the penile urethra and the successful depositing of the sperm in the vagina. (If there is a specific problem then he, too, will visualize it and correct it in his mind's eye.)

Surprising as it may seem, this sort of activity can produce positive results. The exercise need only be done two to three times a day and for only five to ten minutes on each occasion.

Timing intercourse

Having intercourse when a ripe ovum is available for fertilization is more likely to result in conception. Hence the couple need to learn to recognize the time of ovulation (see p.71) and to time intercourse accordingly.

After intercourse the woman should not get up immediately (e.g. to empty her bladder) but try to retain the ejaculate for at least 30 minutes. It helps to place a pillow under the hips so that gravity draws the seminal fluid to the cervix.

Too frequent intercourse should be avoided, especially around the time of ovulation, as sperm take three to four days to mature and become strong and active. Very frequent discharge of sperm can be a natural form of contraception as the sperm are then too weak and immature to reach the fallopian tubes and do their job.

Clothing

To produce normal sperm the testicles should be about 2° Centigrade cooler than the rest of the body – this is why they are outside the body and in the scrotum. A common cause of male infertility is wearing tight clothes which hold the scrotum close to the body, heat the testicles, and interfere with the production of healthy sperm. Changing to loose underpants which will allow the air to circulate round the scrotum should help. For the same reason soaking in hot baths for long spells or any other practice which heats the testicles should also be avoided. Another aspect of this problem is varicose veins in the scrotum. These can increase the temperature sufficiently to inhibit normal sperm production and medical treatment should be sought for this condition.

Drugs

Avoid taking any drugs. Some tranquillizers taken by women cause the prolactin level in the blood to rise so high that ovulation is suppressed. This may be indicated by secretions from the breasts. Some hormones given for premenstrual tension actually inhibit ovulation. It is better to treat premenstrual tension with pyridoxine (vitamin B_6). Alcohol should be limited as too much can affect sperm production.

Any abnormal discharges from the vagina or the penis need medical help to cure the infection.

Irregular menstrual cycles

Women sometimes worry unnecessarily because they have irregular menstrual cycles. They imagine that this is a cause of infertility and if only the cycle could be 'restored' to 28 days they would conceive. This is not true. Whether the cycle is 'every 28 days, like clockwork' or irregular, is insignificant *as long as the woman ovulates*. It is possible to have a 28-day cycle and not ovulate whereas millions of women with irregular cycles who do ovulate are able to conceive. I have even known one woman who had menstruated only three times in her 26 years of life and in spite of having been told that she would never have children, she did manage to ovulate and have a perfectly normal baby. No one knew when she had conceived, nor when the baby was due, but it all worked out well!

Investigating infertility

If conception has not occurred within three to six months then both partners need to be investigated and treatment given to correct whatever problem has been identified.

In an effort to establish and correct the exact cause or contributory causes of infertility, the couple has first to be examined physically to rule out any obvious abnormalities. After that they are examined for specific dysfunction.

Ovulation

One of the first things to establish is whether the woman ovulates. There are several ways of assessing ovulation. One method is to take and chart the basal body temperature (BBT) every morning for a few monthly cycles (see p.101). The woman also records the days when she menstruates and when the couple have intercourse. Although ovulation is considered to take place the day before there is a rise in body temperature, it is now thought that there can be a margin of error of even three days before and after the rise in temperature.

Recording the BBT is a simple procedure and yet it can sometimes strain the couple's relationship. One woman cleverly avoided any problems in the following way:

When I was advised to fill in temperature charts I was lucky enough to have already discussed the problem with a friend in a similar position. I was therefore determined to avoid as many strains as possible that this can put on a relationship because after all, at the end of all the investigations, it's no good if the doctor tells you you cannot have children and your relationship with your husband has suffered because of the investigations.

I decided to make the 'taking of the temperature' ritual as unobtrusive as possible. I left the thermometer on the bedside table ready, within easy reach, and when the alarm went off in the morning, popped it in my mouth for three minutes, then put it back on the bedside table and carried on as normal. After my husband had left for work, or at weekends whilst making the bed, I would fill in the chart, which I kept in the drawer beside the bed. This way life continued as normal and our relationship is still as good as ever some five years later.

Another way of determining whether ovulation occurs is by examining the cervical mucus. A specimen of mucus is spread on a slide and allowed to dry in the air. At the time of ovulation, because of the altered salt content and high oestrogen level, the cervical mucus dries in a fern-like pattern (fern test). For the same reasons, the mucus is also thin, clear and 'stretchable' (see p.102), whereas before and after ovulation the cervical mucus is thick and viscid.

It may not always be easy to establish when or whether ovulation takes place. In such cases an indirect way of finding out is to test for progesterone in the second half of the menstrual cycle. Progesterone is only secreted from the corpus luteum after ovulation has occurred. A blood test, about one week before menstruation is due to start, will show if progesterone is present.

Progesterone also causes changes in the lining of the uterus, and sometimes doctors find it necessary to examine a snip of the uterine lining (endometrial biopsy). This is a simple procedure performed through the cervix and will also be done about one week before menstruation is due to start. Alternatively, the uterine cavity can be scraped out (diagnostic curettage) after the woman is given a general anaesthetic. The scrapings from the uterus are then examined microscopically.

Sperm production

At the same time as the woman is being assessed for normal ovulatory function, it needs to be established that the man is able to produce enough healthy sperm for successful fertilization. This is done by a sperm count from a complete ejaculate. The man has to abstain from intercourse for four to five days and then produce the specimen either from masturbation or coitus interruptus. The semen must be deposited into a clean, dry, glass jar (not a condom as the rubber and chemicals may affect the sperm) and delivered for examination within two hours. This test may have to be repeated as sperm production can easily be affected temporarily by adverse conditions.

If sperm are completely absent in several specimens of semen, then either there is an obstruction in the genital tract or the testicles are not producing sperm. If there are too few healthy sperm, then simple causes like emotional stress, a bout of 'flu or any other illness with a high temperature, tight underpants, etc. may be the reason. The presence of dead sperm in the specimen may be due to infection, antibodies or defective maturation of sperm. It is for the doctor to pinpoint the cause and suggest treatment to improve the sperm count.

Cervical mucus

Once it has been established that the woman ovulates normally and the man produces adequate healthy sperm, the next step is to investigate the normality of the cervical mucus. A post-coital test will indicate whether the cervical mucus is receptive or hostile to sperm. This has to be done just before ovulation is due to take place and when the cervical mucus is normally thin, copious and alkaline. Six to eighteen hours after intercourse, the woman presents herself for examination. The gynaecologist extracts a specimen of mucus from the cervix and examines it under the microscope. If enough live sperm are present then all is well. If, on the other hand, sperm in the cervix are absent or dead but are still alive in the upper vagina, then the implication is that the cervical mucus is at fault. It is either too viscid, or there are antibodies present, or there is an infection which needs to be treated.

The post-coital test may be done before the man has a sperm count because if an adequate number of healthy sperm is found in the cervix then it is reasonable to assume that the sperm count is normal.

Fallopian tubes

Assuming that the cervical mucus is normal, it now has to be verified that the fallopian tubes are open, functioning normally, and that there is no obstruction in the tubes which will prevent the sperm getting to the ovum. Several tests can be done to confirm this.

1. Tubal insufflation involves blowing a gas (usually carbon dioxide) through the fallopian tubes via the cervix and uterus. The pressure is carefully controlled. If the tubes are open the gas passes through them and rises to irritate the diaphragm (the large muscle of breathing which separates the chest and abdominal cavities) causing the woman to feel pain in her shoulder or neck when she sits up or stands up. This test is also done round about the time of ovulation.

2. The uterus and fallopian tubes can be shown up clearly if they are X-rayed while a radio-opaque dye is injected into them through the cervix. Such an X-ray is known as a hysterosalping-ogram and is done early in the menstrual cycle before ovulation and a possible resulting pregnancy.

3. Laparoscopy is a surgical procedure usually done under a general anaesthetic. A small cut is made just below the navel

and a telescope-like instrument (laparoscope) is inserted and directed to the pelvic organs. Through it the gynaecologist can see and inspect the uterus, fallopian tubes and ovaries. Sometimes procedures 2 and 3 are done at the same time.

Treatment for infertility

Treatment for infertility will depend on the result of the investigations and the identified cause of the problem. There are four main types of treatment:

1. Medical – to improve general health and treat infections, antibodies, etc.

2. Surgical – to correct abnormalities in the genital tract.

3. Hormonal – to correct hormonal dysfunction and stimulate ovulation with fertility drugs.

4. Psychological – to instil a calm, relaxed, positive, realistic and yet hopeful attitude in the couple. So often infertility is due only to emotional stress which results in menstrual and ovarian dysfunction or spasms in the fallopian tubes and vas deferens.

Inevitably a great deal of embarrassment, anxiety, stress, disappointment and heartache is associated with infertility investigations and treatments. The following two accounts illustrate poignantly the feelings of two women in such circumstances.

> I never dreamt I would have trouble having children. Growing up dreaming of the day I would marry and have a family of my own just seemed natural to me.
> I had a stillbirth some five years ago which was difficult enough to cope with but felt the best thing would be to have another baby to help fill the desperate void in my life that this experience had left.
> As I had had a caesarean section I was advised to wait six months before trying for another baby. This we did and also decided to get a check-up by a gynaecologist first. Everything

seemed all right so I left hoping to conceive fairly soon.

Six months went by and nothing had happened so I returned to see the consultant who reassured me and suggested temperature charts and to take ——, a particular drug to help the environment in the vagina.

I left again feeling optimistic, armed with thermometer and charts and thus commenced four years of remembering to take my temperature before anything else first thing each morning. I tried to do this as quietly as possible because I did not want the situation to arise where my husband might feel I was only interested in sex at the right time of the month . . .

I returned to the consultant after a few months armed with my charts which felt rather like school reports, i.e. have I got my little x's in the right place? It isn't always easy to see exactly when one ovulates from these charts, especially for the untrained eye. Tensions can be caused by these charts because however hard you try, it always seems as if just at the right time you're either 'too tired', 'got the 'flu' or, because you are aware of the time of the month, tense and therefore end up having a row.

The consultant checked my charts and wasn't sure whether I was ovulating so decided to try a mild fertility drug to encourage ovulation. This I took for two months, then returned again as instructed and because nothing much seemed to be happening, my doctor decided to 'check inside' by means of a laparoscopy.

This was done on a Monday afternoon. I remember coming round, seeing my husband, then the consultant came to see us. He said he thought it would be better if he came back to talk to us when I was less dopey, but I knew from his face something was wrong and persuaded him to talk to my husband who could then explain to me.

Once again our world was shattered. It seemed that after the caesarean I had had a post-operative infection which had done a great deal of damage and it was doubtful whether I could have another baby. He did say there was an operation he could try but he didn't give us any guarantees.

It was bad enough losing our first baby but to suddenly be faced with the possibility of not being able to have any more children seemed too much to cope with.

I had this operation five days later during which a sling was put in to hold up my womb which was tilted so far back it had virtually done a U-turn. There was also some nasty pelvic fluid in which my womb had been lying so this fluid was removed. My tubes were kinked and blocked, also lying in some sort of jelly-like fluid and my ovaries, also in this fluid, were forming hard skins over them. The fluid was removed, my tubes straightened and opened as much as possible, wedge sections opened the ovaries and my bladder was repositioned.

My gynaecologist seemed fairly pleased with the results and informed us that our chances were improved. I now felt more hopeful and tried to think positively.

Three years passed with temperature charts, fertility drugs, injections, blood tests, etc. – virtually everything possible and still no luck so my gynaecologist referred me to a fertility clinic in London.

Once again I was examined and told things looked hopeful and would I come off the fertility drugs for two months and in the second do a cycle of smears myself, then take the fertility drugs for two months, and in the second month do another cycle of smears.

This entailed taking a sample of the mucus in the vagina every other day from end of period to commencement of next. This I did but no period appeared and I had run out of slides so I rang the hospital and was told to bring the slides I had to be checked. This I did and was told the exact day of ovulation and that they thought I was pregnant. I was amazed as that morning I had had some vaginal bleeding and assumed my period was coming. A pregnancy test was done which showed weakly positive and my hormone level checked which showed I was low in progesterone. They said they would treat me with regular injections to counteract miscarriage but not to tell people I was pregnant until, hopefully, my hormone level improved.

I shall never forget that day. I started shaking from head to foot, then dissolved into tears only to be joined by the two nurses present at the time.

Three months passed and my hormones settled down and we were told we could announce the happy event but that I should be sensible and not overdo things and that sexual relations could resume as the danger period had passed.

I now have a beautiful three-and-a-half-month-old daughter whom I keep looking at and still can't quite believe she is mine.

The one thing essential to survive the trials and tribulations of infertility problems is a sense of humour. If you can laugh together at some of the things you have to do it helps relieve some tensions and strains put on your relationship because of this. Especially when it comes to setting the alarm to make love, then rush to the hospital for a post-coital test, sit in a waiting-room full of couples who are all there for the same test, trying not to think about what we've all been up to that morning and keep a straight face. Laughter is the survival valve.

As soon as my husband and I were married we decided to start a family. We were comfortable financially and had a home of our own (and had been living together for one year). I had not been taking any contraception. We used the 'safe period'.

After three months of trying I went to my GP. I told him I was just married but wanted a family straight away. His advice was to go back and see him in one year 'after I had settled into married life'. He also thought that before that time I would more than likely be pregnant anyway – he was wrong.

One year later I went back, asked for a letter to see a consultant whom I worked with and knew personally.

One week later my out-patient's appointment was made. The clinic was fortunately at the same hospital I worked in, and being a nurse and knowing the consultant, I never had any waiting-rooms or waiting-lists to go on. I was treated more or less as a private patient. I worked in the operating theatre at the hospital. The sister of the clinic would phone me to go down as the consultant was seeing his last patient.

My first appointment was rather a surprise. I was told I should have gone to see him the moment I began to 'worry' about not conceiving instead of letting the problem build up in my mind for a whole year. I could see his point. No way did I forget about it and 'settle into married life' as my GP had suggested. I just became more and more anxious as each period came.

I was told to take my temperature every morning before getting out of bed and record this until my next period. Also, if there was a rise in the middle of the graph, roughly fourteen days after my first day of bleeding, be sure to have intercourse.

I was told not to get out of bed after intercourse for any reason, and to place a pillow under my buttocks in order to tilt my pelvis to make the journey for the semen easier – ha! Anyway, no results.

February
The following month I went back to the consultant in the clinic, and one week later I was admitted to hospital for a D & C and insufflation as he suspected blocked fallopian tubes. All was well, both tubes were patent so I was started on oestrogen tablets, one for seven days in the middle of each menstrual cycle at the same time maintaining the temp. charts.

Six months later – nothing. I was becoming desperate. While chatting to a sister at work, I found out that she, too, had been trying for a family for seven years. She had her appendix out and *six weeks* later was pregnant.

August
Well, I had what we call a grumbling appendix for years, so

one night I woke with slight pain in my right iliac fossa and made it out to be rather more than it was. At noon that day I had an appendicectomy (being a theatre nurse for three years I knew what to say when examined and when to say 'ooh'). It turned out that my appendix was rather long and slightly inflamed so it would have been taken out eventually. Anyhow I never became pregnant after that.

November
I was still seeing the consultant every month and maintaining my temp. charts. I was admitted to hospital yet again, this time for a laparoscopy and dye, as my temp. charts were showing that I was not ovulating. I had a small incision made just below the umbilicus and a telescope inserted through this. While the consultant looked at my ovaries and tubes his assistant inserted 20 mls of Methylene blue, the dye, into my cervix which should have passed up through both tubes. However, the results were: both tubes were blocked, both ovaries had cysts around them and the fimbrial ends of both tubes were all stuck with an old infection that I had some years ago but probably not known about. I thought that was my lot. Forget it. You'll never get pregnant. I had worked on patients in hospital with one blocked tube or one ovarian cyst. I had double of everything.

I was so upset and *bitter*. Everyone around me seemed to be getting pregnant – my sister, my cousin, a close friend, a colleague at work, etc., etc. The consultant came to see me. I was rather cheeky. Before he said anything I said 'I know I cannot have a family. I read my notes last night.' (I knew where they kept the staff notes on the ward and while the night nurse dozed off I went into the sister's office and read them. Wished I hadn't as I sobbed all night until my eyes were like golf balls.) He said, 'Serves you right, your notes are private and confidential. Anyway I can put most of your troubles right but it means a major operation but will leave you with a 50 per cent chance of conceiving.' I cried and gave him a cuddle.

January

Admitted again – laparotomy – bilateral wedge resection of ovaries. I had a bikini cut, which pleased me. The cysts were removed. He passed a probe through both tubes and washed both fimbrial ends with hot normal saline to loosen them. I had to be transfused and post-operatively was in bloody agony. The following day a friend visited me. She came into my room looking rather worried. It turned out that she was pregnant. She had conceived with the coil *in situ*. That just about topped everything. On my discharge one of the nurses said 'See you again'. Ha!

February

Another clinic appointment. During these operations I was given a variety of fertility drugs to be taken with oestrogen. I was called in to see the consultant. I knew something was coming. He just sat looking at my notes and temp. charts, then at me. Then he said it, something I had dreaded hearing; 'Nothing else I can do. You're not responding to any treatment. Ovaries not functioning. I've done all I can do.' I just sat there, numb, looking at the floor. Pulled myself together, looked up at him and said cheerfully, 'Oh well. Is that it then?' He suggested my pituitary gland was not functioning properly and he could refer me to a professor at a London hospital for pituitary treatment. The professor, being an expert in endocrinology, might be able to help me, but there seemed little hope. Well I'll try anything, so an appointment was made.

March

Here we go again. I had to start all over again the same treatment the consultant had tried when I first saw him – vaginal smears, post-coital tests, semen analysis, temp. charts, blood tests, the works.

I went back one week later. My husband was OK. I knew that anyway, but it was routine to do a semen analysis before anything (this being his fifth). I saw the professor who informed me that the blood tests I had showed that I had ovulated in March at some time, and there was no doubt, the problem being when as my temp. charts showed no rise at all.

The professor said, 'I would like you to come in next week and have a laparoscopy and dye.' I said, 'I've had one.' He said, 'So? I want to do another one. Patients can have recurrent cysts and blocked tubes.' That did it, goodbye, I never went back. My abdomen already looked like a road map. No more I thought.

April
Friday 14 April, period, regular as clockwork. I did feel down as always when I started my period, but I think I was beginning to accept that I couldn't have children.

At the beginning of May I was ill, *very ill* – headaches, nausea, giddiness, and eventually vomiting, anything and everything, even a cup of tea. I had a week off work (I was now at another hospital as the previous hospital had closed). I began to feel a bit better after that week. Everything subsided apart from vomiting – early morning, every morning. It was awful – on my hands and knees in the loo as soon as I got up. I thought – 'I'm pregnant – no, can't be, it's all in my mind.' I ignored it, but the vomiting continued. My next period was late – unusual for me – I ignored it. It's in my mind. The vomiting continued. I lost 5 lbs in weight. People were saying 'You don't look well.'

One day at work I put a pregnancy test in. I was fourteen days late for my period. I signed the form in the consultant's name – naughty.

I was working a late shift – 1 pm-8.30 pm. At 7 pm I went to supper. When I went back to the theatre a student said there had been a phone call for me. The man had left a number, could I phone back.

It was the consultant's home number. He said, 'Hello, what has been happening with you? What treatment did you have in London?' I replied, 'None, just routine tests.' He said, 'Well, you're pregnant.' I was speechless, lump in my throat, tears in my eyes. I could not believe it. The consultant said, 'Come and see me in the clinic next week.' I put the phone down and literally sobbed.

Is there a connection between infertility and impotence?

Infertility and impotence are two quite separate problems. The man who is infertile is able to perform sexually in a normal way and without any difficulties. His problem is an inadequate sperm count and this only affects the content of the ejaculate and his ability to father children. Infertility does not affect sexual performance and sexual functioning.

Impotence

The man who is impotent, on the other hand, may have an adequate sperm count and is theoretically perfectly capable of fathering children but cannot do so because he has a functional problem and is unable to have sexual intercourse due to (a) his inability to achieve an erection of the penis (b) his inability to maintain an erection long enough to ejaculate.

A distinction is made between the man who has never had sexual intercourse and is said to suffer from *primary impotence*, and the man who had functioned normally, and even fathered one or more children, but later developed one or other of the above problems. This is known as *secondary impotence*.

Causes of impotence
In both types of impotence, the cause is very rarely *physical* abnormality. Mostly, it is a combination of emotional stresses

relating to sexual activity which disrupt the normal sexual functioning. Negative religious and cultural attitudes instilled from childhood also have an effect.

A man is born with the ability to have an erection (this is even seen in very young males). Erection is an involuntary reflex to particular stimuli – either physical or emotional. If the stimuli are positive and rewarding, then they constantly reinforce and strengthen the natural reflex of erection.

Conversely, if erection of the penis is associated with feelings of shame, guilt, or fear of failure, etc., then the erection will subside. If this happens again and again and on every occasion then it reinforces the suppression of the natural reflex of erection. Similarly, if his partner shows contempt, blames him for her own problems, criticizes his performance and generally makes the man feel inadequate as a lover, then the constant bombardment of such negative stimuli will result in secondary impotence with this partner. He may still be able to function normally under different circumstances and with other partners.

It follows therefore that a sexual relationship can be a vulnerable situation for both partners. It tends to flourish best in a relaxed atmosphere of trust, caring, consideration and concern for each other. Positive signals from one's body, one's mind and one's partner are the best ingredients for satisfactory sexual functioning.

There are two other conditions which are sometimes considered to be a form of impotence but in fact they are examples of other forms of malfunction.

As the present barrier methods are the least harmful of all the contraceptives, many new devices will be coming on to the market from time to time to compete with them. Two such examples are:

1. a disposable sponge impregnated with spermicides which is inserted high in the vagina and against the cervical opening

2. a cervical cap, individually moulded for each woman, that can stay in place for about a year

One needs to be cautious, however, about embracing new devices before they have been fully evaluated and given the test of time.

Premature ejaculation

A man with this condition is able to have an erection but is unable to maintain the erection in the vagina long enough for his partner to reach orgasm. Very often ejaculation occurs within 30 seconds of entering the vagina. This is probably conditioned and reinforced behaviour from early sexual activity when, for example, fear of being caught in the act may have caused him to finish too quickly. It is a common problem and may lead to secondary impotence.

Ejaculatory incompetence

This is sometimes called retarded or absent ejaculation. The man is not only capable of having an erection but can maintain it for a very long time, thus enabling his partner to have several orgasms. His problem is the inability to ejaculate into the vagina.

It is believed that the cause is a strong emotional block from some traumatic sexual experience, possibly relating to fear of impregnating the partner.

All these functional disorders can be treated by various forms of behaviour modification with a high expectation of success within a relatively short time.

Will childbirth cure frigidity?

Frigidity is a vague term used to describe a number of female sexual difficulties – particularly the inability to achieve orgasm through intercourse. *Primary frigidity* is the term applied when a woman has never had an orgasm by any means at all – neither from intercourse, masturbation, nor genito-oral play.

Unlike the male, who has to have an orgasm in order to be able to expel his semen into the vagina to father a child, the woman can become pregnant without ever having an orgasm. If a woman was non-orgasmic before her baby's birth, she will very likely continue to function in the same way afterwards. Childbirth is not a cure for orgasmic dysfunction.

Female orgasm

The woman's orgasm is an involuntary reflex to the maximum build-up of sexual tension. It is a response which just happens and is impossible to will or to force. It lasts for only a matter of seconds and the subjective experience is both physical and emotional and varies considerably from woman to woman.

The detailed physiological changes which take place in the genitals and the body generally from arousal to orgasm are of academic interest rather than practical help to the woman with a problem. In fact, it may even distract her from becoming completely involved in the act of love-making if she tries to identify the different phases of sexual response or worries about changes in blood-pressure and heart function. To behave like a spectator – i.e. detach oneself to observe, assess, direct or concentrate on one's performance – is a sure way of inviting problems.

It is usually enough for a woman to know that (a) sexual excitement builds up to a peak which (b) continues to intensify until (c) orgasm occurs and then (d) the body subsides back to the pre-stimulated state. Of the four phases, the first and last are the longest.

The woman's response in a sexual encounter depends on many factors such as:

1. Her attitude to sex as conditioned by personal background, family, religion and society.

2. The possible memory of a traumatic early sexual experience which still haunts her.

3. Previous experience of failure or success regarding orgasm

which has been reinforced over the years.

4. The place and time that intercourse occurs – whether conducive to a warm and relaxed experience, or shoddy, hurried and with risk of distractions.

5. Her attitude to her partner – whether she loves, likes, admires or despises him.

6. The nature of the stimulation leading to the build-up of sexual tension. A woman can easily be put-off if her partner is inept, clumsy, or insensitive to her needs.

7. An inhibited partner, which will inhibit the woman.

8. Fatigue, preoccupation, anxiety, fear of pregnancy, fear of failure to have an orgasm.

Overcoming failure to achieve orgasm

If a woman has consistently failed to achieve orgasm then she needs practical help – neither time nor childbirth will cure her problem. In fact, through repetition her negative response is constantly reinforced and perpetuated. Alternatively, by changing the circumstances that lead to failed orgasm, she is more likely to respond normally.

As sexual intercourse is a mutual activity, any problem which a man or a woman has involves both partners and can only be solved by the couple working together. For this reason the most important factor in overcoming a problem is honest and uninhibited communication between the couple, so that each understands and respects the other's feelings and desires and neither partner criticizes or blames the other. So often problems arise because men and women think and feel differently about sex. They have different aspirations and needs which are unknown to the partner.

The non-orgasmic woman needs to be reassured that there is nothing physically or anatomically wrong with her. Her problem is that she is involuntarily inhibiting a natural and automatic response to the build-up of sexual tensions. She should therefore learn to allow herself to become wholeheartedly involved in an uninhibited way and to allow her body to respond to the sensations she feels. It helps to be self-centred and to concentrate on what *she* is experiencing rather than trying to please her partner. In fact, it is her uninhibited response which will excite her partner.

A woman needs to feel secure in her relationship and trust her partner, otherwise she is on guard and cannot respond normally. She is also sensitive to her partner's moods and attitude and if she feels or senses that he is critical, impatient, exasperated, angry, or stoically controlling himself, etc., then she is unable to function sexually.

Behaviour therapy

The sooner sexual problems are tackled and resolved the better, and if the simple guidelines and suggestions given above are not enough then professional help, based on the principles of behaviour therapy, should be sought. The treatment is graded in stages and both partners have to learn:

1. Honest and positive communication with each other.

2. 'Sensate focus', i.e. each partner in turn learns through touching and caressing the other's body, but avoiding the breasts and genitals, what is pleasant, exciting and sexually stimulating as well as what hurts, irritates, distracts or is unpleasant and should therefore be avoided.

3. The extension of 'sensate focus' to include the breasts and genitals but the couple is instructed to avoid aiming for orgasm. The receiving partner, by placing a hand over the 'giving' hand, indicates the right amount of pressure required and guides the hand to where stimulation is wanted.

Only when the therapist considers the couple ready for it, is intercourse permitted.

Such a programme, properly carried out, is extremely effective and the relearning process takes a relatively short time.

What is vaginismus?

Vaginismus is a spasm of the vagina. It is not just a conscious tightening but a powerful *involuntary* contraction of the outer third of the vagina. The spasm can be so severe that not only is penile penetration physically impossible, but it even precludes an internal gynaecological examination with only one finger.

Sometimes vaginismus is a physical protective mechanism, a form of guarding against being hurt when a woman is suffering from some painful gynaecological condition. Mostly, however, vaginismus is a psychosomatic condition, an obvious example of how emotions can disrupt normal body function. The causes may be fear of sexual intercourse, fear of pregnancy, negative attitudes to sex, or the haunting memory of some early sexual trauma such as rape, incest, etc. – emotional guarding resulting in physical guarding.

It is necessary for the couple to work together to overcome vaginismus under the guidance of a competent therapist. Professional treatment is on two levels:

1. Emotional reassurance, explanation of the condition, and re-education to a positive, healthy attitude to sex.

2. Physical treatment is aimed at very gradually persuading the vagina to dilate and so to relax the spasm. The couple work together – the woman guiding her partner and using fingers or graded vaginal dilators.

In addition to this treatment, it helps to learn physical relaxation of the pelvic floor so that the woman can consciously relax her voluntary muscles in anticipation of being touched, dilated, and eventually penetrated. Using the exercises on p.68 and with the emphasis on 'letting go', this can soon be achieved. The 'visualizing' technique (see p.120) can also be practised with good effect: the woman visualizes the spasm in the lower part of the vagina, and then visualizes it slowly lessening until it disappears and the vagina is completely normal.

This relatively simple form of treatment, properly done, is

highly successful for a very distressing and sometimes even painful condition.

Index